J. Timothy Allen

A Theology of God-Talk
The Language of the Heart

Pre-publication
REVIEWS,
COMMENTARIES,
EVALUATIONS...

"*A Theology of God-Talk* is a much-needed book for all of us who seek to better understand the ways that we speak of and about God. By offering a theology of God-talk as the language of the heart, this book creates for the church a means of conversation, which helps to articulate the realities of ordinary lives. The book demands that we examine our practices, structures, and images of God, through our use of language. Most importantly, it is a much-needed volume that moves all of us toward refashioning (or reframing) the psychosocial symbolic order to include a theological construct that speaks to persons across a broad spectrum of theological perspectives.

Allen places his work within the context of pastoral care, with particular attention given to persons experiencing crisis. Through incisive and creative analysis, Allen constructively derails notions that have often served to minimize the importance of our God-language. The distinctiveness and power of the book comes through Allen's skillful ability to narrate the interrelated textures of linguistic praxis within a pastoral context. *A Theology of God-Talk* will serve as a valuable resource for all who engage in the practice of ministry, as well as those teachers of theology who are charged to prepare persons to share in the life of clients and parishioners."

Rev. C. Anthony Hunt, DMin, PhD
Executive Director,
Multi-Ethnic Center for Ministry
of the United Methodist Church

More pre-publication
REVIEWS, COMMENTARIES, EVALUATIONS . . .

"Allen probes understanding the God-language used by sufferers and comforters. This is a superior study undergirded by the sagacity of the Bible, the insights of such notable writers as Madeleine L'Engle, C. S. Lewis, and John Macquarrie, and a plentitude of anecdotes. Allen urges caregivers to be attentive to the God-talk employed by sufferers, to seek the meanings of their God-expressions, and to examine how they as consolers utilize them as well. Allen discusses how God-talk is often misunderstood, and that what is needed is the study of the remarks of sufferers and the reframing of the simple similitudes often offered in reply. Clergy and other caregivers will find Allen's study a thorough, valuable, and most practically helpful treatment of a topic so inevitably important to all."

Peter E. Roussakis, PhD
*Academic Dean,
The Graduate Theological Foundation,
Donaldson, IN*

"In addition to his own ministerial encounters, J. Timothy Allen has extensively researched the topic of God-talk. He has found that sufferers, especially in times of crisis, view their experiences with head and heart—appearing to give a rational and irrational interpretation of the same event. Sufferers' God-talk is explored in the biblical context, through rational explanations, and narrative that may be mythic, historical, or literary.

For this pastoral counselor, the most valuable admonition received was that caregivers first seek to discern what the suffering person needs when the 'Why, God?' question is posed or when God is cast as benefactor or villain. Pastoral caregivers need to refrain from giving answers that are theologically correct according to their understanding of God. Instead, they need to learn to listen to God-talk on many levels: not only through their intellect, but also with empathy in order to create liminal space where the sufferers can safely explore their God-talk and find healing for their pain."

Ann V. Graber, DMin
*Distance Learning Coordinator,
Viktor Frankl Institute*

"Allen's thesis is that there is 'a mythical, spiritual, wisdom-like meaning behind the God-talk uttered in the throes of grief.' In his book, *A Theology of God-Talk*, he presents his own biblical perspective about what this meaning might be. Theoretically and practically, Allen is relentlessly loyal to the mystery of the sufferer's religious experience and to the not-to-be-fathomed mystery of God. He takes issues with 'educated caregivers' who dismiss as theologically ignorant those who say, for example, 'God took Uncle Harry yesterday.' Allen pleads with pastoral caregivers to allow sufferers the space they need to use metaphorical language to express their difficulties. Then, he counsels, invite sufferers to use imagination to find thir way to new meanings and images of God.

More pre-publication
REVIEWS, COMMENTARIES, EVALUATIONS . . .

"I found the book insightful and challenging. Allen's style is sometimes shocking and evokes dialogue. He does not hesitate to take on those he finds guilty of the 'philosophical and theological laziness' that fails to properly interpret and appreciate the way sufferers talk about God.

The book will be useful to all who provide pastoral care to folks in crisis. It will serve as a source of lively discussion and insight in theological reflection seminars in clinical pastoral education learning settings."

Jane Litzinger, MA
*Chaplain and ACPE Supervisor,
Wake Forest University,
Baptist Medical Center,
Winston-Salem, NC*

"Allen, an experienced parish pastor, has written a challenging book for pastors who offer care to those in crisis. He argues that the pastor must pay close attention to the inchoate, but deeply theological, God-talk spoken by the person in the midst of crisis. Pastoral caregivers often hear expressions of anger or remorse as they care for people in the midst of life-changing circumstances. Allen argues that most pastoral caregivers dismiss these utterances or try to redirect the person to a theology more acceptable to the pastor.

As a hospital chaplain, I found myself intrigued with Allen's arguments. Indeed, as people experience crisis, they want to find meaning, and often their expressions of faith are troubling to the theological worldview of their pastoral caregiver. Allen provides a thoughtful framework through which to understand that sufferers' God-talk is both consistent with Scripture and helpful to the one in crisis. I found Allen's chapter on God-talk and Apocalyptic particularly absorbing. As a teacher of pastoral care in the hospital context, I appreciated his discussion of ways caregivers can assess their parishioners' use of apocalyptic language. Allen has helpfully pointed to ways that this language can help bring sustaining hope to those experiencing traumatic loss. At the same time, the author rightly suggests that pastoral caregivers stay alert to ways that this talk may signal a denial of reality.

I recommend Allen's *A Theology of God-Talk* to pastoral caregivers, both parish pastors and chaplains. I look forward to those in our discipline continuing to discern ways that we can hear the God-talk of those who are in crisis and respond most helpfully. Allen has offered a helpful foundation for those discussions."

Elizabeth Stroop, MDiv
*President, North Carolina
Chaplains' Association;
Associate Director,
Department of Pastoral Care,
UNC Hospitals,
Chapel Hill, NC*

NOTES FOR PROFESSIONAL LIBRARIANS AND LIBRARY USERS

This is an original book title published by The Haworth Pastoral Press®, an imprint of The Haworth Press, Inc. Unless otherwise noted in specific chapters with attribution, materials in this book have not been previously published elsewhere in any format or language.

CONSERVATION AND PRESERVATION NOTES

All books published by The Haworth Press, Inc. and its imprints are printed on certified pH neutral, acid free book grade paper. This paper meets the minimum requirements of American National Standard for Information Sciences-Permanence of Paper for Printed Material, ANSI Z39.48-1984.

A Theology of God-Talk
The Language of the Heart

THE HAWORTH PASTORAL PRESS
Religion and Mental Health
Harold G. Koenig, MD
Senior Editor

New, Recent, and Forthcoming Titles:

Adventures in Senior Living: Learning How to Make Retirement Meaningful and Enjoyable by J. Lawrence Driskill

Dying, Grieving, Faith, and Family: A Pastoral Care Approach by George W. Bowman

The Pastoral Care of Depression: A Guidebook by Binford W. Gilbert

Understanding Clergy Misconduct in Religious Systems: Scapegoating, Family Secrets, and the Abuse of Power by Candace R. Benyei

What the Dying Teach Us: Lessons on Living by Samuel Lee Oliver

The Pastor's Family: The Challenges of Family Life and Pastoral Responsibilities by Daniel L. Langford

Somebody's Knocking at Your Door: AIDS and the African-American Church by Ronald Jeffrey Weatherford and Carole Boston Weatherford

Grief Education for Caregivers of the Elderly by Junietta Baker McCall

The Obsessive-Compulsive Disorder: Pastoral Care for the Road to Change by Robert M. Collie

The Pastoral Care of Children by David H. Grossoehme

Ways of the Desert: Becoming Holy Through Difficult Times by William F. Kraft

Caring for a Loved One with Alzheimer's Disease: A Christian Perspective by Elizabeth T. Hall

"Martha, Martha": How Christians Worry by Elaine Leong Eng

Spiritual Care for Children Living in Specialized Settings: Breathing Underwater by Michael F. Friesen

Broken Bodies, Healing Hearts: Reflections of a Hospital Chaplain by Gretchen W. TenBrook

Shared Grace: Therapists and Clergy Working Together by Marion Bilich, Susan Bonfiglio, and Steven Carlson

The Pastor's Guide to Psychiatric Disorders and Mental Health Resources by W. Brad Johnson and William L. Johnson

Pastoral Counseling: A Gestalt Approach by Ward A. Knights

Christ-Centered Therapy: Empowering the Self by Russ Harris

Bioethics from a Faith Perspective: Ethics in Health Care for the Twenty-First Century by Jack Hanford

Family Abuse and the Bible: The Scriptural Perspective by Aimee K. Cassidy-Shaw

When the Caregiver Becomes the Patient: A Journey from a Mental Disorder to Recovery and Compassionate Insight by Daniel L. Langford and Emil J. Authelet

A Theology of God-Talk: The Language of the Heart by J. Timothy Allen

A Practical Guide to Hospital Ministry: Healing Ways by Junietta B. McCall

Pastoral Care for Post-Traumatic Stress Disorder: Healing the Shattered Soul by Dalene Fuller Rogers

Integrating Spirit and Psyche: Using Women's Narratives in Psychotherapy by Mary Pat Henehan

Chronic Pain: Biomedical and Spiritual Approaches by Harold G. Koenig

A Theology of God-Talk
The Language of the Heart

J. Timothy Allen

The Haworth Pastoral Press®
An Imprint of The Haworth Press, Inc.
New York • London • Oxford

Published by

The Haworth Pastoral Press®, an imprint of The Haworth Press, Inc., 10 Alice Street, Binghamton, NY 13904-1580.

© 2002 by The Haworth Press, Inc. All rights reserved. No part of this work may be reproduced or utilized in any form or by any means, electronic or mechanical, including photocopying, microfilm, and recording, or by any information storage and retrieval system, without permission in writing from the publisher. Printed in the United States of America.

Text excerpted from "Dear Mackenzie: A message to my granddaughter" by Robert McAfee Brown. Copyright 1994 Christian Century Foundation. Reprinted with permission from the March 2, 1994 issue of the *Christian Century*. Subscriptions: $49/yr. from P.O. Box 378, Mt. Morris, IL 61054.

Cover design by Anastasia Litwak.

Library of Congress Cataloging-in-Publication Data

Allen, J. Timothy (James Timothy), 1959-
   A theology of God-talk : the language of the heart / J. Timothy Allen.
     p. cm.
   Includes bibliographical references and index.
   ISBN 0-7890-1514-5 (alk. paper)—ISBN 0-7890-1515-3 (alk. paper)
     1. Pastoral counseling. 2. Language and languages—Religious aspects—Christianity. 3. Suffering—Religious aspects—Christianity. I. Title

BV4012.2 .A45 2002
253.5—dc21
                                                          2001045678

In memory of Miss Dawn Cooke

ABOUT THE AUTHOR

J. Timothy Allen, MDiv, MA, has served Southern Baptist and United Church of Christ congregations as a minister since 1981. He earned a BA in religious studies from the University of South Carolina at Columbia, an MDiv from Southeastern Baptist Theological Seminary, and an MA in religious studies from the University of North Carolina at Chapel Hill. He is currently completing a PhD at Graduate Theological Foundation. He has presented papers at Society of Biblical Literature regional meetings and the American Academy of Religion regional and national meetings.

The Reverend Allen teaches religion at Randolph Community College in Asheboro, North Carolina, and has published articles in the *Journal of Pastoral Care, Prism (UCC), Preaching, Pulpit Digest,* and *The Christian Ministry,* as well as three books. He and his wife, Chaplain Jackie Allen, live near Burlington, NC.

CONTENTS

Preface and Acknowledgments   ix

Introduction   1

   God-Talk As Reframing   4
   Examples of God-Talk   7
   Purpose of God-Talk   12
   Methodology for Interpreting God-Talk   17
   God-Talk As the Tension Between Belief and Reality   20

Chapter 1. Typical Responses to God-Talk   27

   The *Christian Century*   28
   Madeleine L'Engle   34
   Martin Marty   40
   C. S. Lewis   47
   Rabbi Harold S. Kushner   50

Chapter 2. Theology, Myth, and Imagination in God-Talk   57

   John Macquarrie's God-Talk   57
   The Exclusion of Myth in Theology   64
   Myth and the Religious Imagination   69

Chapter 3. God-Talk and the Storms of Life   73

   Responses to Storm-Talk   75
   Spiritual Dynamics of Survivors   77
   Biblical Examples of God-Induced Storms   78
   Storms As Agents of God's Plan   82

Chapter 4. God-Talk As Myth   91

   God-Talk, Myth, and the Confrontation with Evil   91
   An Exploration of Myth   101
   The Biblical Creation Myth   107

Chapter 5. God-Talk and Apocalyptic — **111**

- What Is Apocalyptic? — 111
- Where Does Apocalyptic Come From? — 114
- The Bias Against Apocalyptic Language — 119
- How Apocalyptic Works in Pastoral Care — 124
- Biblical Images for Pastoral Apocalyptic Interpretation — 126

Conclusion: Genres of Faith — **131**

- God-Talk and the Genre of Tragedy — 132
- God-Talk and the Genre of Prayer — 134
- God-Talk and the Genre of Story — 138

Notes — **143**

Index — **157**

Preface and Acknowledgments

The following pages present a (not *the*) theology of the phenomenon of God-talk. They are the culmination of nearly fifteen years of experience, reflection, study, and conversation. The information presented here has been enhanced by the suggestions of various chaplain friends and feedback from ministerial colleagues. While the conclusions presented here are finally my own, they have been greatly influenced by others in the pastoral fields.

My approach has been experiential, phenomenological, biblical, and theological, generally in that order. I have taken the phenomenon of God-talk within the experience of grief and tragedy and explained it theologically by exploring its parameters biblically. Although this discussion is Christian in scope, the conclusions may also be informative for those of other faith traditions.

The reasons for this study will be discussed in detail in the Introduction, but a brief explanation is offered here. When someone employs God-talk such as "God took Uncle Harry yesterday," I have witnessed too many educated caregivers dismiss such words as being theologically ignorant. I once thought this way too until I encountered God-talk in an intense two-week span that brought me three funerals in three days and four within two weeks. It was in this trial by fire that I began to understand this ritualistic language that arose in times of doubt and despair. Over the next few years I began to see that there was a mythical, spiritual, wisdomlike meaning behind the God-talk uttered in the throes of grief. What was lacking, however, was an adequate theological interpretation of this phenomenon. In the pages that follow I have produced an initial, practical theology, a grammar if you will, of the phenomenon of God-talk, the language of the heart.

Many people have offered encouraging words, pointers, and even criticism along the way. Chaplain Jane Litzinger was the first to offer an interested ear. Chaplains Charla Littell, Janet Forest, and Paul Fulks also gave wonderful advice. Ministerial friends such as Norman Harris, Larry Williams, Jody Wright, and Brian and Melissa

Hatcher, offered support and solid criticism. There are others, Chaplain Barry Morris among them, who have used these observations about God-talk in their own ministry and suggested a few improvements for the conclusions presented here. A note of thanks also goes to Reverend Lynne Hinton, pastor and emerging novelist, who stroked my ego greatly when she related that my article on God-talk as myth was one of the most informative she had read during her days of clinical pastoral education.

My thanks to Chaplain Richard Hunt at Wayne Memorial Hospital in 1995 who invited me to speak to his chaplains about God-talk. I was also invited to speak on the topic of God-talk at the fall meeting of the North Carolina Chaplains Association in 1994. The comments and criticism from both of these organizations helped me to clarify much of what follows in these pages. Also, the staff chaplains at Burlington Regional Medical Center, Burlington, North Carolina, listened to and offered suggestions concerning my ideas about God-talk. These conversations are also reflected in the following pages.

I also owe a great debt to Orlo P. Strunk Jr., PhD, editor of *The Journal of Pastoral Care,* for taking a chance and publishing three articles on the subject of God-talk. The first article, "God-talk and Myth," appeared in the winter 1992 issue. A second installment, "Genres of Faith," appeared in the spring 1995 issue, and the article "God-Talk As Apocalyptic" was published in the winter 2000 issue. Each of these articles appears in the following pages. The first has been modified somewhat, while the last two are reproduced here nearly verbatim. Thanks again to Dr. Strunk and the journal for permission to reproduce these articles in this work.

After the publication of these articles, I received several comments from readers and friends. Their observations were quite helpful and have increased the quality of the conclusions presented here.

Special thanks goes to Dawn Marvin who, despite a Christmas flood, an injured foot, a cancer-laden father-in-law, a hysterectomy, and a new puppy to boot, still managed to use her computer skills to save me much grief and keep my religion intact. Gracious thanks go also to my wife, Chaplain Jackie Allen, who has endured too much God-talk conversation over breakfast, lunch, and dinner.

Much gratitude is offered to the folks at Haworth Press. Their editors were always available and their attention to detail saved me from much embarrassment.

A final word of thanks goes to the churches I have served in a pastoral role since 1987. While the members of Damascus Congregational Christian Church (UCC), Liberty Vance United Church of Christ, and St. John's New Mission UCC have grieved and questioned the various despairs of life, they also tolerated my propensity to objectively analyze their God-talk and their spiritual needs. Their patience and understanding have allowed these pages to be written and given to others. I trust that their griefs and my ponderings upon the God-talk that emerged from their crises will prove fruitful to those who must confront the God-talk of others in their daily ministries.

Introduction

Ministers and other pastoral caregivers confront God-talk on a daily basis. Some of the God-talk comes in the form of statements such as "God just doesn't like me anymore" or "God took Uncle Harry today" while others rise such as "I don't know why all of this has happened to me now but I guess there is some reason for it." Depending on the context, we may dismiss some of the statements, but others must be considered carefully as we administer pastoral care. Deep within such responses lie a person's theology of and experience with God that are quite pertinent to the crisis at hand, thus they must be handled with care and not dismissed as just irrelevant babble or evidence of improper theology.

Often within God-talk we can locate a dilemma facing the person. For example, in the previous statements we find the belief that there must be a divine reason for the current affliction in their lives. The sufferers are looking for a rational reason for a seemingly irrational event in their lives. This implies that, for the sufferer, God is for some reason and in some way involved in the present affliction. The dilemma may really be that the person believes that God is ultimately good. Why, then, would a good God do such terrible things to a person? For those who are curious about how God-talk works, we see another potential problem: the world of reason, where everything is supposed to make sense, clashes with real life, where we all know that very little makes sense. In academic terms we see the conundrum between rational and irrational thought.

From the previous scenario we also see that God-talk irrupts in the liminal time of crisis and tragedy and thus interrupts ideal, rational, reasonable theology that is espoused in everyday life. In this chaotic interruption in our lives, some of us resort to rational theologies and explanations of suffering because that is how we are trained to handle life, yet, as we will come to understand, tragedy is a quite irrational, temporal time of life where irrational thought seems to make more sense. This dilemma spells out our first observation about God-talk that informs the following discussion: We are exploring God-talk which manifests itself in times of crisis where the irrational supersedes the rational.

Regarding the first example of God-talk mentioned previously the speaker may think God is angry with him or her because of something done in the past. Pastoral probes from the caregiver might find no "original sin" and thus the speaker might be led to see no connection between the incident and the past. On the other hand, in the case of a diagnosis of lung cancer, the sufferer might fully understand how his or her two-pack-a-day habit has brought about God's anger. This leads to a second observation about God-talk: Personal perception plays an important part in the use and the interpretation of God-talk.

Through such use of God-talk the sufferer is tacitly telling the caregiver, "If I can just understand the reason behind this turmoil in my life, then I could better get through the tragedy by understanding it or by learning to place more hope in my God." This belief permeates the use of God-talk and leads to yet another observation: The spiritual recovery and survival of the sufferer during the time of crisis depends upon the questions in and the answers to the God-talk voiced by the sufferer. For this reason we will examine God-talk as spoken by sufferers and what it means for them and those who provide care for them.

This book is based upon my own ministerial work with sufferers in times of crisis. My experience with this phenomenon with both sufferers and ministers who reach out to them as well as friends who offer "words of comfort" has provided me with a renewed appreciation for God-talk. Along with this, I have witnessed far too many times how caregivers take a one-size-fits-all pastoral theology and methodology and apply it to the God-talk confronted in a particular crisis situation. This quite un-pastoral approach neglects the uniqueness of the person manifested in their life story, personal theology, and religious background. It also ignores the social, academic, and spiritual context of the sufferer. These various facets of the sufferer often determine how we should respond to their voiced theology during the time of crisis.

For example, in many instances caregivers are so focused on the *sufferers* that we forget that the spiritual, theological, and pastoral dynamics are totally different for *survivors*. I noticed this during the days after Hurricane Andrew devastated southern Florida. One newscast showed a video of what was left of a neighborhood. As the camera panned down the suburban streets, the viewer was introduced to house after house that lay in ruins. Then, however, out of all this chaos stood a vestige of hope: one lone house remained intact. Spray painted on the plywood that covered the windows was the phrase "Jesus Saves." One can certainly understand the exuberance of this survivor in this expression of praise and thanks, but many viewers and ministers I talked to were appalled at the insinuation of the phrase. How could the home owner say such a thing when the neighbors' houses were destroyed?

The discussion concerning the theology implied in this phrase reflects the particular focus of the pastoral caregivers. They worried about the insinuation that Jesus "saved" only this house while apparently destroying the others. Why did this family merit favor from an apparently fickle God? What did those less fortunate do to tick off God? Was God really involved in such a capricious choice as this phrase implied?

We can certainly understand such reactions. In the midst of such tragedy, we are focused on the pain of the sufferers. But this attitude displays a one-sided approach to God-talk and, consequently, it reveals a lack of understanding concerning the spiritual need for God-talk for all concerned in the time of crisis. Caregivers often focus on the language of the sufferers, but survivors should be allowed to put their faith response into words, too. Survivors, who must deal with such issues as the guilt of salvation, are searching for ways to voice the confused elation they feel deep inside after a tragedy. The words they attribute to God for their particular predicament provide some kind of perspective to their survival.

Thus, we will examine the specific context of God-talk and suggest ways to view God-talk in order to see it from various perspectives. These perspectives will help caregivers recognize and investigate new ways to understand and interpret the God-talk being used. This hermeneutical process will also help ministers and counselors respond better to the God-talk encountered in pastoral situations not only of sufferers but also of survivors.

We should also understand that in the context of pastoral care, God-talk is not just confined to our clients and parishioners. Caregivers often, and sometimes subconsciously, use God-talk in their daily walk either to understand the predicaments around them or to interpret them in order to console others. For example, how many times have we said to someone, "The Lord will take care of you during this time of grief?" This type of God-talk may soothe a seething soul or it may come across as trite, depending on the situation and the presentation of the speaker and the mood and faith of the listener. The implication here, of course, is that God really cares about us during times of tragedy. As ministers, both lay and ordained, we certainly believe this faithful assertion, but we have no scientific proof that such a Presence will come to this person. Questions, therefore, abound. Why do we speak for God? What if God does not want to be with this person? How do we really know that God cares for *this* person? Thus, our God-talk makes claims for God just as the God-talk we encounter implicates God in various ways. As caregivers, we, too, need to be aware of our God-talk, its implications, its unspoken assumptions, and its uses.

GOD-TALK AS REFRAMING

As part of our introduction to the dynamics of God-talk we must learn to reframe its parameters. For example, one phrase that consistently occurs in times of grief and one that many criticize is this: "The Lord will not put on you any more than you can bear." The phrase reflects a solid biblical foundation. In Genesis 22:1-3 we read quite clearly that God tested Abraham. Paul, perhaps leaning upon this belief, voiced similar concerns in 1 Corinthians 10:13 when he counseled that God will not place any more temptations upon us than we can handle. Whether temptation or testing, the Bible makes it clear that God is involved in some way and that God does not mete out to us any more than we can handle. Thus, this God-talk phrase stands upon solid biblical precedent.

Those who criticize this positive thinking look upon the phrase as cruel, however. It implies that God is directly involved in the present tragedy and thus is testing us to see how much we can handle. I, like others, have responded to such God-talk with questions such as "What kind of God would do such a sinister thing?" But I have found in my experience that, for those who have faith, this implication is entirely true. This revelation comes not only from my own experience but from those who have survived tragedy with their faith intact as well as from biblical stories. On the personal side, parishioners tell me that the phrase, while sounding simple and uncomfortable to them during the tragedy, makes a lot of sense once the crisis is over. Once on the other side of the tragedy, those who were once in despair have found the joy of relief from the pain and suffering of their particular tragedy. Having survived the tragedy and, holding to their belief that the Creator is in control of the Creation, they then realize that God indeed had not put on them more than could be handled.

When analyzed in this way, we see that this phrase now makes sense to them because they have found it to be true. While it may sway haphazardly on the lines of theological or philosophical reason, it is experientially true for the user of God-talk. The faithful sufferer, strengthened with the armor of faith, can indeed survive anything. Thus this phrase reflects a very reasoned faith, and this kind of God-talk serves a healing purpose in time of suffering.

As can be seen from the previous example, part of the process of understanding God-talk involves taking the time to explore the biblical ramifications of what is implied or suggested in the phrase. We see that this phrase is biblically accurate when we understand Paul's interpretation. As one who survived shipwrecks, floggings, stonings, resentment, misinterpretation and scorn, not to mention a tinge of guilt concerning his persecution of Christians, Paul continued strong in his faith. He of all people knew quite well the implications of this belief. The key here is that Paul *chose* to believe God was with him during all of this persecution.

Paul survived his tragedies and persecutions because he chose to see God's will as somehow directing his life through these events. He used these experiences to inform him and change his existing theology to fit with new and ever changing circumstances. Paul's trust in God helped him to view tragedy with such a positive, faithful, healing outlook. Others, however, may not choose such a positive route. They will see despair in such events and thus declare, "I simply can't cope with such a burden." Here we see no hope and, as we will eventually see in later chapters, the key to surviving tragedy and thus interpreting the ensuing God-talk from that tragedy is hope. The task for the caregiver, then, is to be familiar enough with all aspects of the faith tradition in which I would include the Bible, hymnody, theology, and the folk tradition of God-talk, to guide the sufferer to the positive route of healing faith.

What is involved in understanding and utilizing God-talk in the pastoral encounter is termed "reframing" the issue. Pastoral theologian Donald Capps sets out for us a methodology of reframing that I will use throughout this work. Thus we need to briefly explore this method and its importance for understanding God-talk in the pastoral conversation.[1]

When pastoral caregivers encounter a person in crisis, questions arise. Often these questions center around "Why?" and this implies to the caregiver that an answer is needed. Capps argues that although "Why?" has been the focus of traditional pastoral care in the past, we need to change the question and move more to "What?" in order to get at the real issue involved in the personal dilemma.[2] In order to do this he suggests that we need to see the pastoral conversation in two tiers of first and second order change. First order change occurs within a system that itself remains unchanged. Second order change alters the system in order to bring about change. Capps notes that while first order change works in many pastoral encounters, it does not bring about effective change in others. In order to rectify this problem, the opposite of what would normally be suggested or accepted in the counseling situation is offered by the caregiver.

Part of the problem, Capps notes, are the definitions we use in our pastoral care. For example, there are difficulties and then there are problems. "Difficulties are a fact of human existence," Capps informs us. Difficulties are what we label suffering, evil, and death. Problems are "situations that are created and maintained through the mishandling of difficulties."

For the phenomenon of God-talk we will see that this distinction is very important. For example, seminaries and divinity schools train students in the "problem of evil" with the implication that evil can be "solved" if only we can apply the right theology through the proper methodology of reason. Death is likewise termed as "evil." Sufferers and pastoral caregivers thinking in this vein thus approach suffering as if it can be solved, eliminated. According to Capps, however, this approach is incorrect. Suffering, death, and evil are simply facts of life. They are difficulties, not problems. Capps warns us that where we go wrong is in treating them as problems instead of difficulties.

When we mishandle difficulties and treat them as problems then we are, in effect, introducing even more problems into the already confused crisis situation. We will see that people today often feel as if they should not have any difficulties at all. Others misapply theological assertions to their problems and thus create more confusing scenarios. Some simply misinterpret theology either out of biblical ignorance or for their own personal convenience. The overall effect, according to Capps, is that we try to achieve a utopian state where "we might attain perfect happiness or solve the unsolvable." Since this can never happen, difficulties are made more problematic for both the sufferer and the caregiver.

In essence, what must be done is to put into effect a paradox that forces the sufferer to see his or her situation in a new frame. In the specific situation of God-talk, the normal "frame" is this: Why would a loving God do such a thing to me or allow such a disaster to happen to me? The frame is that we consider God loving and good. There is nothing inherently wrong with these depictions of God. But our present social and cultural mindset has confused this notion of a loving God because of very limited ideals and definitions about what "loving" and "good" entail.[3]

In order to put into effect what Capps calls a second order change, the opposite of the "normal" frame must be introduced. In the case of God-talk, then, we need to suggest in the counseling situation the most obvious conclusion based on the sufferer's perception of the current crisis as evidenced in the God-talk: maybe God is not good and loving according to our understanding of these terms.

Capps warns that second order change "usually appears odd, *un*commonsensical, unworkable and impractical." But this is entirely necessary when the obvious, sensible solution is not helping to alleviate the painful issues at hand and indeed is, in fact, only exacerbating them. We will see throughout this book that following the "uncommonsensical," as Capps puts it, is the key to understanding God-talk.

EXAMPLES OF GOD-TALK

My interest in God-talk began during a particularly intense period of ministry. It was during this time that I began to analyze the varied uses of God-talk during times of pastoral care. For instance, I talked with a family who survived a fiery plane crash in Iowa and counseled their relatives. The crash survivors repeatedly said, "I don't know why God selected us to live and others to die. God was just with us that day, I guess." They had a very good point because people both in front of them and behind them died in the crash. The fuselage broke right behind them, allowing them to escape while others remained trapped in the burning wreck. Given such factual parameters, what other conclusions could they draw?

We see in this God-talk the two basic questions Capps spoke of in his discussion. The "Why?" question looms in the forefront of this God-talk and thus the caregiver would lean toward trying to answer the question or noting that the question simply cannot be answered at all. But the inherent question is "What?" What will this family do with the guilt of their salvation given the grief and loss of others around them? What will the family do now that they are alive? And within these "what" questions are implications of purpose. Since they were saved by God, as they firmly believed, then what should they do with their new life? Here we also see a shift from the question of "Why?" to a question of "Who?" Who is behind all of this and what does this mean for me?

During this same year my parents survived the devastation of Hurricane Hugo. Within the reports of the damage related by many survivors I constantly heard stories that began or ended with "God must have been in that hurricane last week. How else could those trees have fallen around our house and not hurt anything?" My first response to these thoughts was, "How could anyone think that God would just willy-nilly pick and choose who would receive destruction and who would get off scot-free." But as I struggled with these questions I began to see another parameter of God-talk that underlies this discussion: there is a *pastoral purpose* for God-talk specifically within the context of the crisis. It was with this experience especially that I began to see that caregivers need to understand that God-talk serves a specific and necessary purpose that should be recognized and respected.

Again, Capps would argue that this purpose is couched in the second order change question of "What?" What is the purpose of our salvation? What is the reason we were spared the devastation that hit our neighbors? Thus, the purpose of God-talk is to provide a guiding and sustaining foundation for faith. This faith believes that there is a purpose to the event, and a purpose raises the concomitant question of "Who is involved here?" If there is no purpose, no answer to "What?" that can be found, then all is left to Chaos. There is no order to life at all.

Along with this, in just two weeks I did my first funerals as a pastor, three in three successive days and four total during that time. A fifty-year-old man died suddenly of a heart attack while working in his backyard. Although shocked, the family told me they were glad God took him quickly. "That was the way he wanted to go," the family said over and over. In other words, it was as if God had taken this man according to his wishes. In examining this pastoral context I asked myself, "Is this a way of saying that God answers prayers?" This thought opened up a new question: Does God always answer our prayers according to what we want? What about the family whose loved one was not "taken" according to their prayers?

These questions, however, neglect the fact that this God-talk phrase has already moved past the "Why?" to the "What?" The sudden and tragic grief experienced by this family was alleviated, though not altogether removed, by the "what" of their God-talk. It also opens up the realm of myth: their God-talk had created a myth—that God takes people according to their wishes.

A middle-aged woman who was a respected real estate developer and was noted for her numerous acts of community kindness as a volunteer died after a short bout with cancer. Many of her friends asked before, during, and after the funeral, "Why couldn't this have happened to another person? She was such a good woman. There must be a reason for this." Of course, this God-talk implies that bad things only happen to bad people. Despite the classist insinuations and even the implicit arrogance behind such beliefs (Does God only mete out bad things to the poor? The wicked? The disrespectful?), this type of thinking reflects a basic Old Testament tenet manifest in the plot of the Book of Job. Why *do* bad things happen to good people? Do good things happen to bad people? On the other hand, modern interpreters of life may ask another question: What if what happens to people both good and bad should be seen as just an event, neither good nor bad?

This line of questioning reveals Capps' warning about confusing difficulties with problems. Once we try to answer the "Why?" question we begin to chase theological rabbits everywhere all the while missing the more relevant question of "What?" What of this woman's good works in the community? What of her dignified death with cancer? In trying to solve the "Why?" questions we may miss out on celebrating the joyous aspects of the sufferer's life.

An elderly woman died after a twenty-year illness. Her daughter sighed and told me that "I just placed it in the Lord's hands. If God wanted her to die, then so be it. God knows what he is doing. Who am I to argue with him?" Again we see God's providence proclaimed in a statement of faith during a time of grief. We also see the personal release by the caregiver of the sick woman into the providential hands of God, which is a basic ritualistic function of religion in general. Pastoral caregivers often counsel sufferers to release things that we cannot control and live within the limitations of our own created humanity. This woman's God-talk certainly seemed to indicate her compliance to this advice.

The one story that touched me greatly during this heightened time of pastoral care concerned a fourteen-year-old female leukemia patient who died suddenly after a successful bone marrow transplant. While we may allow ourselves to move on to the "What?" questions regarding elderly people or folks who have lived a full life, the sudden, unexpected death of a young person brings about more "Why?" questions than other tragedies. During this time of grief nearly everyone said to me, "She's better off up there now. She had suffered for so long. I'm glad God had mercy on her and stopped her misery." Given the many tragic ups and downs of her brief life, I had to agree, even though I was not comfortable with the implications of the God-talk. There certainly seemed to be a kernel of truth, not to mention a spiritual sigh of relief, in the God-talk.

As I look back on this God-talk, however, I realize that the "Why?" questions were simply too painful to even voice. The God-talk seemed to move the sufferers to the more relevant question of "What?" at the expense of dodging the more acceptable question of "Why?"

These are the personal examples from my ministry that triggered my initial investigations of the phenomenon of and the meaning behind such God-talk in pastoral contexts. Some other examples reveal more of the issues and implications that I have just presented. For instance, during an evening newscast, in a telephone interview with a person who chose to ride out Hurricane Bonnie on Oak Island on the North Carolina coast, a man responded when asked why he chose to stay on the island, "If it is my time to go, then it is my time to go." Although we may be tempted to see a stubborn lunatic behind such a statement, his words reveal a deep, if perhaps hard-to-understand, trust in God's providence. Would our faith allow us to make such a final stand fully trusting in God's care? People who live on the coast and have to deal with hurricanes and storms yearly may understand this belief better than educated caregivers called upon to interpret their disconcerting God-talk. It is not right for us to impose our theology upon people without fully understanding their personal context of faith.

On the lighter side, NASCAR racing phenomenon Jeff Gordon is no stranger to the winner's circle. His strong faith in God is also no secret to his fans and to the racing circuit. After a victory he always gives credit to God. "It's just our time to win. God has been very good to us." Questions abound for us after such a response. Does God listen to prayers of athletes and let one person/team win? Is this preferential providence? What of the other competitors? Did their prayers not merit enough of God's attention to cause a win? Does Jeff Gordon have more pull with God than Rusty Wallace, Mark Martin, or Kyle Petty? But such questions miss the boat altogether. If we see this God-talk as an act of praise, however, then we can compare this to similar phrases in the Bible, especially the Psalms, in which God is given credit for various victories the psalmist experienced. Is not an athlete allowed a time for praise to his or her God for the joy of victory despite what we think is a misappropriation of praise?

This phenomenon of God-talk as praise can be seen in the tragic realm as well. For example, when terrorists bombed the American embassy in Nairobi, Kenya, in 1998, Abraham Muthogo Kamau was in the Ufundi House next door. The blast from the second explosion hurled him into the street, causing him injury while saving him from the building debris which toppled onto and killed other innocent victims. A passerby took him to the hospital. The next day he explained why he was alive. "God loves me."[4]

Of course we might immediately ask why, according to such theological logic, God didn't love the others who died in the senseless blast. Such questioning reveals that we are not involved in the context of this survivor. Many caregivers, however, even though trained in empathic caregiving, overlook or even ignore the particularities of the immediate context and instead mistakenly present pastoral care from a perspective that misses entirely the message that is being given. To what else would a survivor attribute his miraculous salvation? If we dare to enter the realm of the mystical, we might even ask more penetrating questions. Isn't it just a bit odd that *he* was thrown into the street by the second blast while *others* were not? If we attribute this miracle to Fate, as pastoral theologian Wayne Oates warns against, then we have unwittingly removed God from the picture altogether and put our faith in the latest modern deity, Luck.[5] If we approach sufferers and survivors with such secular methods, then why do we call ourselves *pastoral* caregivers? Pastoral care should offer a divine alternative to traditional psychotherapy and sociological counseling. God-talk opens a door to such a pastoral conversation.

The paradoxical nature of God-talk can be witnessed in reactions to the tragic murders of the Columbine High School students. In the national edition of the *United Church News,* we see a local pastor's response to the tragedy: "God didn't do this." But in the very same publication one of the Columbine faculty who survived the tragedy proclaimed, "I see God in the Littleton tragedy."[6] Here we see the very tension that will be explored throughout this work: educated caregivers offering rational, technical, and "correct" theological interpretations of tragedy to those whose experience of the tragedy suggests a very different explanation. I will argue throughout the following pages that this form of God-talk as voiced by the sufferers is indeed the more realistic depiction of God because it is, as Capps says, "uncommonsensical," unworkable, and impractical. It forces us into the very second order change that is necessary to move properly through the grief process.

PURPOSE OF GOD-TALK

Such situations and language are not new to ministers and pastoral caregivers. We hear this kind of God-talk all the time. When we explore the deeper implications of these phrases, we find most center around the question "Why?" This haunting question, which is also the basis for the biblical lament as evidenced in the Psalms and in Lamentations, implies a purpose behind the tragedy or incident. This raises an immediate flag for some caregivers because in our scientifically-influenced psycho-therapeutic training we are taught rational approaches to tragic problems. In our ministerial training we work through arguments of theodicy (the justice of God), the problem of evil and the concomitant notion that God is good and, therefore, God is not involved in evil in our world. Yet, as Howard W. Stone remarks, pastoral caregivers, when faced with the lament *why* in the heat of a personal crisis, suddenly seem to shift their focus, withdraw, or just ignore the question altogether. Despite our rational, academic training, we somehow refrain from looking for the purpose behind the deity's action implied in the God-talk.[7] Capps would observe that we are stuck in first order pastoral care.

Notice, however, that this God-talk does not even entertain the thought of *whether* there is a purpose. The God-talk, by its very use, indicates that the one caught in tragedy at this moment hopes God is very much involved. If God is not, then what? Does Evil have me caught in its snares? Is Chaos this rampant on earth? The sufferer hopes that God is indeed very involved in the present tragedy because the other options simply open up too many potentially threatening possibilities. In Capps' terms the other options turn difficulties into problems. The pastoral caregiver should approach the issue this way: If tragedy were all around you, who would you want at the controls, God, who at least has the potential for doing good and caring in a loving way, or Evil, the Devil, Chaos, or Fate?

Thus, according to the God-talk voiced in the heat of the crisis, there is no doubt for the sufferer who is involved in the tragedy. The real question for the speaker, then, is, as Capps points out, "*What* is the reason or purpose behind this current experience?" This distinction is very important for caregivers to make. As we will see, responses of caregivers and interpreters of tragedy often assume there is no purpose, but when we examine their response carefully, we see that they, too, ironically believe in a God who is in overall control of life. If God is in control of life in general, then doesn't that mean God is also in control of both weal and woe? The prophet Isaiah was bold enough to believe in such a view as he spoke words of encouragement to those who suffered in Babylonian exile.

> I form light and create darkness,
> bring prosperity and create disaster,
> I, the LORD, do all these things.

(Isaiah 45:7 NIV)

Interestingly, the Hebrew words for "prosperity" and "disaster" are peace *(shalom)* and evil *(ra)*. The God who creates the world creates peace and evil too. The prophet offers these paradoxical words of "comfort" to the Israelites after they have seen their beloved Jerusalem and its Temple destroyed by (the divinely appointed!) Babylonian army, after they have lived in captivity in Babylon for nearly fifty years, and just as they are about to journey through the desert once more to live in the Promised Land that now lays in ruins. These pastoral words are certainly meant to put into effect what Capps would call second order change.

The Psalms present both the loving and the punishing side of God in pastoral songs. While God's goodness is often extolled, some psalms suggest otherwise. For instance:

> We are consumed by your anger
> and terrified by your indignation.
> You have set our iniquities before you,
> our secret sins in the light of your presence...

Yet within this song of pain and repentance comes a paradoxical ray of hope:

> Satisfy us in the morning with your unfailing love,
> that we may sing for joy and be glad all our days.

(Psalm 90:7-8,14, NIV)

Biblically speaking, to have only weal without woe, love without wrath, is an inconsistent picture of God. Such a theology presents dangerous pitfalls for those of faith. Caregivers must be cognizant of these manifold sides of God. In Chapter 1 we will explore more fully how learned people often respond to tragedy. By examining their own God-talk, we will see that, while they disparage God-talk that implies

God is involved in their tragedy, their own God-talk implies that they subconsciously believe God is very much involved in the ups and downs of our lives.

Many people cringe when such a conclusion is offered, and I have witnessed this response in numerous ministers who react the same way when God-talk erupts. "How could such a loving God do such a thing?" many respond. Notice that, while fighting against the implications of the God-talk before them, they, too, have resorted to their own brand of God-talk to respond back. Their response implies that they believe a *loving* God does not cause such tragedy. But this response is also a form of God-talk. While some God-talk implies that God is involved in tragedy, other God-talk just assumes that God only does *good* things. This, too, is an implication that many tend to make. We tend to forget that the Bible, full of inspiration from people who pondered such eternal questions long ago, states emphatically that the Lord is God of both Good and Evil.

For example, this loving God demanded that Abraham offer his only son as a sacrifice. This test of faith, as Genesis 22:1-13 plainly says, goes against the grain of today's sensitivities, but it also implies that God's love goes beyond our understanding of good. This loving God destroyed an entire Egyptian army in order to save the Israelites from certain death. God's anger rose against Israel so God "incited" King David to sin through the imposition of a census of Israel (2 Samuel 24:1). This text was so theologically rife with complications that the writer of Chronicles rewrote it and blamed Satan for the sin (1 Chronicles 21:1). One reading of Ezekiel reveals that the God of Love sent the Babylonians to destroy Judah for its sins but that this God of Love also took care of the exiles in Babylon and, through Ezekiel's pastoral work, began to paint a beautiful picture of a new day for the Israelites. The loving God we want to believe in hurled a great wind to toss Jonah about on the sea in order to get him to repent of his refusal to go to Ninevah. New Testament writers remind us again and again that God sent Jesus to die a cruel, forsaken death on a cross for our sins. The Book of Revelation offers pastoral hope to the persecuted believers by reminding them that, in the last days, God will deliberately send destruction upon the earth and unleash Satan's powers for a while so that peace and love may reign supreme on earth. These few examples alone reveal that there is more to God's goodness and love than our current limited notions of love and goodness suggest.

At issue here is how we have dodged the sticky issue of theodicy by replacing it with our own notions of how the deity should act. Theologian Frederick Sontag has correctly called to task those who resort to anthropodicy, the placing of human values and emotions upon God. "We have all been apologists for God too long. How do we know God wants us to argue to free him from all responsibility for evil?" He points out an important conundrum for those who only emphasize God's love: "If we claim God's nature to be controlled by love, we only heighten the tension, since evil and destruction in the world are hardly evidence of love." He goes on to note that those who have survived tragedy experience what Capps would call a second order change. "If one lives beyond such a total death experience, a new view of life and God is bound to result. Most obviously, all easy and sweet views of God disappear. . . ."[8]

There is more to the issue of God-talk, however, than the purpose behind the tragedy, and for this reason, we will not take the time to explore the complicated issues surrounding the theodicy debate. As we are beginning to understand, there is a personal, pastoral purpose for God-talk itself. Thus, caregivers need to learn to ask, "What is the purpose of the God-talk I am encountering?"

For example, in order to check the theology being spoken to me during such pastoral contexts, I would listen to similar comments after the time of tragedy and occasionally bring them up when no such talk was being offered in our general conversations. Invariably, the God-talk would disappear after the chaos of the tragedy dissipated and the folks would revert back to what I would call their "normal" theology (God is good, God does not do such cruel things to us, etc.), but when the conversation shifted back to the tragedy, then the God-talk would invariably and unapologetically appear again. Puzzled by this phenomenon, I asked people in the course of regular conversation if they really believed that God would do what was implied in their God-talk. Most, when confronted with the contradictions, retreated to a more standard use of God images. It then became clear to me that there was a *purpose* to the use of God-talk during the time of crisis and once the purpose was clear then I began to see *how* God-talk was used in our everyday and temporal theology, and how its theology was in fact more in agreement with biblical notions of the Creator's dealings with Creation.

Once the purpose and use of God-talk became clear to me, I began to notice particular verbal and theological patterns in the God-talk. Some of it came in what I would call short stories while others appeared in outbursts that could properly be labeled prayers, to mention two examples. Theologically, the God-talk often looked for or implied a reason for the crisis and removed any possibility of Chaos or Evil or the Devil having any part in the experience. Once these parameters were understood, then I located biblical counterparts of the God-talk. Much of the God-talk, while seemingly questionable to many in the pastoral fields, simply repeats long-held religious beliefs or replicated theologies that, when checked out thoroughly against the biblical stories, remained true to the biblical depictions of God. Thus, I realized that what was said or implied in God-talk was, in a deeper spiritual sense, biblically and, therefore, theologically true, and how people respond to this God-talk often indicates how biblically literate or illiterate they are.

METHODOLOGY FOR INTERPRETING GOD-TALK

In a search for comparisons to the phenomena of God-talk and its implications, we find numerous parallels that help us in our quest to better understand God-talk. These parallels are often found within the Bible itself. For instance, we can compare God-talk with simple proverbs, creation stories, myths, tragedies, and thus stories, along with similar categories such as prayer. Often, however, we can find informative parallels to the responses of pastoral caregivers in the discussions between scholars of religion and biblical studies on how to interpret biblical categories. For example, the current debate concerning apocalyptic literature centers on how some scholars consider apocalyptic and its users as second-class religious citizens. I have observed this same reaction in ministers when confronted with apocalyptic imagery in a pastoral context. This evaluation should come as no surprise since ministers and pastoral caregivers are trained in seminary in the methods and interpretive approaches outlined in biblical commentaries and introductions that all too often disparage apocalyptic literature and its adherents. Given this training, caregivers would therefore easily and uncritically adopt the bias of these scholars. Thus, the discussions of certain interpretive approaches for scholars will prove helpful to ministers who, in their everyday work, also interpret various religious texts from the oral, pastoral tradition.

For our purposes here, God-talk comes in distinct patterns that fall neatly into literary categories, what I call "genres of faith." The word *genre* implies a literary approach to this phenomenon, and this will be evidenced throughout this work. Charles Gerkin has pointed out that each person is a "living human document"; thus, we need to interpret that life as if it were a text.[9]

Similarly, God-talk resembles literary texts to the point that we can incorporate the methodologies used to interpret literary genres in our approach to God-talk. For example, I will contend later that all God-talk depicts God mythically; thus, we need to be familiar with the literary genre of myth. To understand God-talk as myth we must acknowledge that myth describes something that cannot be explained and understood using rational, scientific methods. We should understand that all God-talk assumes, perhaps even creates, a "mythology" about God. When we say that "God took Uncle Harry" or that "God does not place on our shoulders any more than we can carry," we are entering the realm of myth. We can't scientifically prove that God really does this, but we can believe God does this because it certainly *seems* as though God acts this way. In many instances, believers simply apply religious beliefs, such as those found in the Bible, to their situations to create a mythos incorporating various God-talk scenarios that help them interpret and thus survive the present tragedy. In other circumstances, however, it will be clear to the pastoral interpreter that a myth has been incorrectly and dangerously made. Here a judgment must be made by the caregiver concerning intervention into the sufferer's world of fantasy instead of myth.

We cannot prove any of the implied beliefs that are presented to us in pastoral conversations but we know for sure that sufferers and caregivers can and do believe in them. Therefore, we must understand the category of myth and how it works within the religious world of the believer if we are to fully appreciate what people are saying when they revert to this usage.

Other God-talk can be considered as short, spontaneous prayers. An outburst such as "Oh my God!" should not be viewed as just an excited exclamation but as what it really is: a brief and intense prayer. In many instances families that do not consider themselves religious at all will be found repeating such phrases over and over again without even thinking of their actions or implications. While possibly annoying to those in the caregiving ministry we should ask: Is this the hurting soul crying out? Such short prayers may indicate a deep, yet neglected need for God, or they may reveal that these people really do want to believe in God. A later conversation that focuses on this experience may lead the family back to church and God.

Other short prayers can be examined as well. The outburst, "Why is this happening to me?" implies that the speaker believes that Someone (God? The Devil?) is doing something to him or her. Attentive caregivers should begin asking questions, either out loud or to themselves while caught up in such distress. Who is this Someone? Why is it assumed that this Someone is out to get this person? Does the sufferer understand what he or she is saying? Along with this, is the sufferer ready to accept such implications and what they mean for further faithful living? Is the sufferer willing to accept this purpose for this tragedy?

Some God-talk resembles tragedy, as in the ancient Greek genre of play writing. There is a method to the literary genre of tragedy that is useful to understand when confronting tragic God-talk. Tragedy comes just when life is going great or on the rebound again. Sitting on top of the world, the sufferer is pushed off the mountain of joy into the valley of the shadow of death. Thus, phrases such as "Just when I got my life back together again God knocked me down once more" can be understood and interpreted within the larger framework of tragedy.

Some God-talk can be examined as if it were story. Here we need to understand how the imagination works in our souls. Perhaps there is a spiritual need for us to believe that God will work out a fairy-tale ending to our tragedy. Learning to employ the question of "What if . . . ?" will help us to explore the ramifications of such God-talk. For example, if someone says that God took little Susie from this earth, caregivers can then ask the sufferer, "What if that were so?" Allowing the sufferer to imagine how and why God would do such a thing might bring about much-needed healing or expose the flawed ending in such a story.

In other instances God-talk comes across as if it were apocalyptic prophecy. "God will get that drunk who killed my boy!" is a violent response to a terrible tragedy. "Your time is coming buddy; you'll get what you deserve!" is another typical response heard by ministers and caregivers. Such God-talk implies an eschatological time of retribution that will come to the perpetrator of the tragedy. The belief that God will vindicate the just through violent means is a mainstay of apocalyptic literature. Such literature arises during times of despair when all other forms of religious thought have proven empty. Unfortunately, as we have already noted, many view apocalyptic literature as the belief of the ignorant or conservative person (these two are often incorrectly lumped together). We will see that the biblical interpretation of and use of apocalyptic is quite intellectual and is based on hope, not gloom and doom. Hope is certainly necessary during times of tragedy and is a mainstay of effective pastoral care.

Overall, when we step back from the pastoral encounter and analyze God-talk it looks and sounds like short, wise aphorisms or proverbs that have stood the test of time. The phrases immediately arise during times of grief when sufferers are lost for words to say. It is as if they resort to an unconscious, maybe even archetypal, collection of spiritual wisdom or theological folklore during times of tragedy and despair. It has been my experience that wise pastors or respected folks in our faith communities pass on to us these pithy words of comfort during times of suffering, and we in turn pass them on to others.

Along with this folkloric understanding, when I began to analyze this type of God-talk, I discovered that it is often the very brevity of God-talk that often calls the phrases into question. Much like when we read proverbs or folklore and smile and say to ourselves, "If only life were that simple," many look at God-talk and think the same thoughts. As we are beginning to realize, however, when we look beyond these brief sayings and probe deeply into their biblical underpinnings, we find they reflect much wisdom and biblical theology.

GOD-TALK AS THE TENSION BETWEEN BELIEF AND REALITY

The previous examples of God-talk reveal that we must be careful in our attempts to categorize and label God-talk. Just like the chaos we encounter in times of tragedy, God-talk often does not make sense or come in consistent ways. Many similar beliefs were espoused throughout the history of Israel and the early church and were recorded in our scriptures. Not all of these beliefs are consistent in their theology or their depiction of God. For example, Old Testament scholar Walter Brueggemann notes that the editors of the Old Testament were quite content with placing contradictory and ambiguous depictions of God side by side. He writes "the text, taken as a whole, seems to have no sustained interest in sorting matters out or bringing to resolution many of the contradictions that mark both Israel's faith and Yahweh's character." Concerning the topic of theodicy Brueggemann claims the Old Testament does not seek to resolve this complicated question. He goes on to state that "There is in Israel's God-talk a remarkable restlessness and openness, as if each new voice in each new circumstance must undertake the entire process anew."[10] This should help caregivers understand that, from a biblical and therefore theological standpoint, the God-talk we encounter in pastoral situations is not supposed to be consistent or even make sense at all times. Ambiguity, irony, paradox—all mainstays of literature—abound in the context and text of God-talk as well as in biblical stories and theologies, and comparisons of these phenomena reveal similarities that will help us better interpret God-talk in our ministry. God-talk, just like its biblical counterparts, arises out of specific situations where particular theologies proved necessary for the security of the current social, economic, political, and religious structure. Studying disagreements between biblical texts should help us put aside the incorrect and nonpastoral idea of a consistent picture and theology of God. Two examples of such ancient beliefs illustrate this point.

As mentioned before, throughout most of the Bible, there is the persistent and generally comforting belief that if one does good, one will be blessed by God. This belief is especially implied throughout the Books of Deuteronomy through Kings, and it is implied in their counterpart books of the prophets. It is also a dominant theme in the Book of Proverbs. If the ancient believers would simply do what God instructed them to do, then good in the form of blessing, wealth, and respect would follow. Today this idea is still popular as evidenced by what we teach our children. If one does good as in getting a good education and obeying the laws, then one will do well in life. One will live well, have a good job, bear respectable children, and be a positive force in one's community. We should admit that most of the time this belief system works quite well. Those who stick to this dictum tend to live prosperous, contented, respectable lives.

There are, however, some whose good lives have not reciprocated in good fortune. They are the epitome of goodness, but their lives are filled with tragedy. The writers of Job and Ecclesiastes explored this contrary notion. Job was the epitome of "those who do good will be blessed," and it is evident throughout the Book of Job that he based his whole belief system on this very promise. Despite his goodness, however, Job lost everything that manifested God's blessings when God made a questionable bet with the Satan[11] that Job's faith could endure any tribulation that came his way. This tragic, ancient story is retold day after day in the news, in church vestibules, and in front of caregivers and for those who take the time to learn from it the story tells us that, while we pawns may do good all of our life, we have no guarantees that the gods will return the favor as they battle each other in the chess matches of life.

Ecclesiastes approaches the matter from a different angle and it too debunks an ancient and modern myth. We are generally taught that those who do well and prosper will be happy. Their lives will be filled with joy as they enjoy all things they have acquired. This is not a worship of materialism. Remember that the Bible as well as popular myth teaches that, if one does well, one will be blessed and the ancient manifestation of blessing was wealth and happiness. The writer of Ecclesiastes, however, instructs that, although we do well and are the model of success, we may still not be happy, and God may be the reason why (Ecclesiastes 6:1ff.)!

There is more to life than doing things well and living well in the middle of our accumulations. Indeed, the life of simplicity, the very opposite of what we are taught to achieve, is the desired goal according to Ecclesiastes. Many today prove true the ancient words of Ecclesiastes in their search for a simplified lifestyle after a life lived chasing the American dream of climbing corporate ladders fourteen hours a day.

Interestingly, both Job and Ecclesiastes are placed by scholars in the genre of wisdom literature, which is also where the Book of Proverbs along with selected psalms and biblical stories are placed. Job and Ecclesiastes were written by people who survived physical or psychological tragedy and thus have a whole new perspective on life.

Life lived on the other side of terrible tragedy produces a new and entirely different theology, one that is not comfortable to those of us who still live on the front side of tragedy.[12] Thus, we will use the biblical wisdom literature as a paradigm for our exploration of God-talk. While most of the world uses the popular and often consistent belief of do good and God will bless as found in Proverbs, others who have suffered and survived tragedy, along with those who have learned from such sufferers, know of a more profound way of life, one that James Fowler would no doubt list as the highest on his scale of spiritual human development.[13]

It should be quite apparent by now that this discussion and examination of God-talk involves two distinct approaches: biblical and phenomenological. I have taken experiences and looked to the Bible for parallels that are informative for pastoral care. There is a basic pastoral reason for this. Time and again when I have been called upon to enter a tragic situation, I have encountered people with Bibles in their hands or biblical stories and verses on their lips. The first chapter illustrates this point very well. In times of tragedy, faithful people, and people who want to be faithful, turn to their Bibles for some word from God. Sometimes this need is demonstrated by turning to the pastor who is supposed to embody the Word of God. In either instance, we need to become more familiar with the scriptures and their implications for spiritual care in our everyday caregiving.

Along with this, the fields of theology, psychology, pastoral care, and relevant areas of religious studies, such as mythology and phenomenology will be consulted to help us better understand the greater phenomenon of God-talk. This multidisciplinary approach will help the caregiver to understand the God-talk encountered in the pastoral experience.

I end this Introduction to the problem and interpretation of God-talk with a story that is indicative of the process I have used. The best explanation of how God-talk is usually criticized by pastoral caregivers and, ironically how it can be understood by caregivers, came to me when I presented this information to a group of chaplains and ministers. For the majority of caregivers the initial reaction to the previous conclusions is polite, professional interest along with either theological agreement or disagreement. The reluctance, I have discovered, arises because of two things, both of which are related. First,

I have observed that many ministers and chaplains have an extremely limited experience with the Bible. Thus, their biblical literacy is minimal. The reason for this is twofold. Seminary graduation requirements often allow only a small number of biblical courses along with other required courses in church history, theology, counseling, and languages. Thus, a minister or counselor can graduate with only a cursory knowledge of the Bible. Also, many second career ministers are coming to seminaries with little or no exposure to the scriptures. Thus, the problems become more pronounced. Along with this, those trained in counseling are likely to use their extra course hours not for biblical courses but for other classes in counseling, human development, family systems, and issue-related counseling theory. Thus, what is already a minimal exposure to biblical stories is whittled down even more.

The result? When confronted with God-talk that does not fit within their limited God-view, caregivers may retreat to conventional theology rather than work to understand the image within the whole array of biblical theologies available. Focused on only one or a limited number of God-images learned from experience or in seminary, they simply cannot or do not want to confront the different, confusing, and paradoxical depictions of God. Unfortunately, such reactions can result in limited, first order pastoral care for those who are suffering.

Second, most ministers are trained to accept and incorporate a particular view of God into their personal pastoral ministry. This is usually broken down into a conservative or liberal interpretation of how God acts and why. But this dichotomy is not entirely accurate. The real culprit in understanding God-talk is that many caregivers also carry in their pastoral baggage a notion of good and bad things that God either does or does not do. Most God-talk, I have noticed, depicts God doing "incorrect" things, and thus is rejected as being deficient or reflecting a primitive belief in God by pastoral caregivers who tend to image God in more "correct" ways. But as we will see, God-talk spoken by the sufferer often reflects accurately the biblical characterization of God. In other words, it is theologically quite "correct" depending on when and how it is used.

Thus, when I presented this information to a group of chaplains, I could tell that many were not convinced. Then one chaplain spoke up. Her story embodied the very crux of the matter and the basis of the discussions throughout this book. She told of a family having a wreck on the interstate near her home. The mini van the family was riding in hit a pothole and swerved across the median and flipped over, killing the passengers. Questions that all pastoral caregivers are familiar with arose concerning the incident. Why did it happen? Why to this particular family? What did they do wrong? Why did they have to die because of somebody else's negligence? All of these questions imply some divine motive when analyzed.

The chaplain who related this incident told the group that, after the wreck, she looked with disdain upon those who tried to find some sort of divine motive in this incident. She, like many of us, was trained in our Enlightenment-influenced psychology and pastoral care in which philosophical reason and rational theological arguments such as the problem of evil and theodicy overrule deeper, mystical interpretations of life to the point that mystery is replaced with understanding, and faith is lost to the expense of truth.[14] Her initial pastoral assessment of the matter was to leave God out of the tragic picture altogether. Scientifically speaking, the event could be explained rationally (roads break down; road crews failed in their jobs; the driver should have been paying closer attention to the conditions of the road, etc.), and thus God should be left out of such discussions of "natural" accidents. As she confessed to the group, she, like many of her peers, simply saw and interpreted this tragedy as an accident that could randomly happen to anyone at anytime. "Surely no good God would cause such an event to occur," she said to our group. Most of us would agree with such a rational interpretation of this tragedy.

Ironically, however, in just a matter of weeks this chaplain was traveling with her family on the same interstate and, at the very same spot, she too hit the same pothole and her mini van swerved across the median and flipped over, replicating exactly the same accident that had previously claimed a whole family. The chaplain and her family, however, survived and this presented her with new questions involving not only guilt and survival but also Providence. Now she was in a different perspective from which to make observations about tragedy. On the surviving end of the tragedy her pastoral interpretation was now different. Why? By all rational arguments she should have died. But now she was on the *other* side of tragedy looking back rather than on the front side of tragedy looking ahead. She had stared Death face to face and survived. She had confronted the fact that she could and maybe should have died. The questions she asked herself concerning the accident were filled with implications. Why, at this very same place, in the same type of accident, did she survive while the other family died? Was she better than the other family? Was there a purpose for her life and not a purpose for the other family? Here we can see her shift into second order thinking as outlined by Capps. Her "Why?" was now turning into "What?"

As this chaplain and then tragedy survivor honestly related to the rest of the largely unconvinced group, she understood very well the observations that I present here. Given *this* set of circumstances, there *had to be* a reason for her surviving the same type of accident that only weeks before had claimed the lives of a whole family. The reason she came to accept in order to understand this tragedy was that she simply had more to do on earth. And it was this conclusion that helped her work through the guilt and other emotions that came with her crisis.

Whether we agree with her conclusions is not the issue. My contention here, and throughout this work, is, *as long as the implications and conclusions arrived at in the use and understanding of God-talk in the time of crisis are not impeding the emotional and spiritual health of the sufferer or survivor, they are serving a unique and spiritual need.* It is our task as caregivers to understand this phenomenon and use it in our care of others.

The preceding discussion presents the focus for the remaining pages. The religious phenomenon of God-talk will be explored using biblical and religious methods in order to better understand why and how God-talk is used. In the following chapters, I will set out a theological grammar for God-talk, the genre of faith, the language of the heart.

Chapter 1

Typical Responses to God-Talk

In the Introduction we encountered and briefly examined several examples of God-talk. We applied Donald Capps' method of reframing to these pastoral phenomena and examined them in regard to what he called second order change. We learned that God-talk often hints at or assumes second order change. But one question remains for us here. Why do pastoral caregivers frequently misunderstand God-talk in this way? One answer is the resources that counselors and sufferers refer to generally utilize first order language. Their thoughts on suffering are important and helpful, but they generally do not ask, and sometimes even evade, the questions that would allow a move to second order change. Thus, the sources we ordinarily look to for guidance in times of tragedy unwittingly make problems out of difficulties, to use Capps' terminology.

In this chapter we will explore in greater detail some of the typical learned responses to God-talk by people whose thoughts on suffering have garnered much respect from and informed many pastoral caregivers in their approaches to grief and tragedy. Several different sources were chosen for examination and all represent a responsible, intellectual and passionate approach to the interpretation of suffering by fellow sufferers. These theologians and writers cover the theological gamut from liberal to evangelical and represent Christian and Jewish backgrounds.

This discussion of typical responses to God-talk reveals why pastoral assessments fall short of understanding the language of the heart. We will also find that, paradoxically, those who deny the validity and theology of everyday God-talk reveal in their own words that they actually believe the implications of the very God-talk they have just refuted. Thus their criticism of God-talk reveals their own deep spiritual need for the healing comfort God-talk can bring when used and understood correctly. This chapter then should prove that God-talk and its peculiar implications of how God deals with humanity is a necessary part of grief reactions and that it reflects a genuine need of the soul to express itself in times of suffering.

THE CHRISTIAN CENTURY

The *Christian Century* is well known for its academic slant in the world of Christian religious reporting. Its editors and writers pen much of the groundbreaking and transformative religious ideas that effect religious trends in America. Ministers and theologians benefit from its publication and, if we look through its pages, we can learn much about how God-talk is perceived and interpreted in the academic and ministerial world.

In a stimulating pastoral offering, Robert McAfee Brown wrote a letter of consolation to his granddaughter Mackenzie who hovered on the brink of death shortly after her birth.[1] While working through his own questions of suffering, he struggles to answer the universal question of why one so young is being placed near the brink of death so soon. Along with this he wonders, if she is to die, what good has her short life brought to this earth. His questions are typical of those asked by all sufferers, yet his rational responses are typical of those offered by caregivers in that they appear cold and limit the providence of God.

In the midst of his grief he writes, "I want to believe that God does not play cat and mouse with us, at least not interminably." Notice the struggle between what he now believes and what the evidence seems to reveal within his hurting heart. This is an erudite way of stating what many sufferers blatantly say in the midst of tragedy: "Why are You doing this to me?" While Brown says he "wants" to believe that God does not do such things to us, we can clearly discern from his question an internal struggle and possibly even a trusting desire to accept the latent belief that God really is doing this to little Mackenzie.

Brown reflects the deep question most sufferers must confront in their own time of turmoil. It is far easier to deny God's involvement in our suffering and make up a theology that fits our beliefs. This is the method followed in Rabbi Harold S. Kushner's *When Bad Things Happen to Good People*.[2] Theologians, ministers, and even pop psychologists probe the reasoning behind the God who does or does not do such evil things to us. But we do not have the option to make up a new theology of God. A quick reading of the Bible, especially the Psalms, reveals many descriptions of God doing things, both good and bad, to people. These stories and hymns were not written on a whim by "primitive," nonacademic theologians. Instead, they were carefully penned with the wisdom of hindsight and much reflection about the indescribable ways of an apparently whimsical, capricious, yet loving Deity. The fact that they were selected as scripture, as informative for our spiritual growth, should lead us to understand their value and truth for our religious questions. Their theology makes us confront the very real possibility that God is very much at work in our lives, creating both weal and woe, as Isaiah prophesied centuries ago (Isaiah 45:7). We are not free to deny God's power to direct our lives in whatever direction the Divine Will leads. Instead, we must learn to accept what comes our way, and then we must work to understand the theology that comes with such acceptance.

Brown's personal reflections on Mackenzie's illness reveal that, whether she lives or dies, he believes her life has already given something to this world and therefore has served a purpose in the larger design of Creation. Such observations reveal that, deep within his heart, he feels her young life has a purpose. This understanding of her life poses yet another question. Does this not imply that God then has some purpose in her life as well? If so, then aren't believers allowed to step out in faith and imply that God was behind Mackenzie's illness if it "widened the circle of love" and "deepened the mysteries of love" and affirmed "the realities of love" as Brown asserts in his own version of God-talk? Who but God can reveal such mysteries through the short life of a little child? If little Mackenzie's life brought on these deep, profound realizations to Brown (and to us through his writing), then, looking back with the wisdom of hindsight and standing at some distance from the emotions of grief, her illness indeed could be said to come from God since it has served the very Divine Purpose of bringing more love to this earth.[3]

It is this line of reasoning that is reflected when many opine that "God must have a reason for this accident" or "there is a reason for this, and we will understand it one day." They are trying to find some salvific purpose to an act that, on the surface, appears cruel and unjust. Their God-talk does not make light of the sufferer and the present tragedy but focuses on a future hope and salvation from suffering that will come to fruition one day.

Brown writes about the mysteries of life that appear when we suffer. "What has happened to you is bad, and yet good has come of it."[4] We could probably safely suggest that Fate, Chance, or even the Devil would never bring about a calamity that eventually ended in good. But certainly God can turn tragedy into goodness. Once again, we see a hint of God's providential hand in the tragedy as betrayed by Brown's own words. This would make God the God of Good and Evil, which is exactly what the Bible says about God.

Some point to the cross of Christ as an example of bad turned into good. What the Jews or the Romans meant for evil (to rid Judea of this troublesome itinerant teacher), God meant for good. But this interpretation of Jesus' death misses the point too. The Gospels consistently focus on Jesus' determined journey to Jerusalem to fulfill the will of God manifest in being handed over, persecuted, killed on the cross, and then resurrected. In Mark 8-10, for example, we read three times how Jesus predicted his impending death to deaf ears. He even struggled with this death, this "cup" as he called it, just before his time to die (Mark 14:32ff.). All of these passages clearly demonstrate that Jesus knew the cross was meant for good from the very start.

This is not to suggest that grief and tragedy are to be greeted with jubilation. The Bible certainly teaches us to cry and also rejoice in the proper season. Jesus' own struggles with his death on the cross reveal that sadness and tremendous grief come along with a greater good. Tragedy catches us off guard and humbles us with its unexpected arrival. Indeed, we will see in a later section on God-talk and tragedy that the humbling experience may be one of the Divine Reasons for tragedy in life. But the previous statement by Brown reveals one of the more popular assumptions of the modern world: suffering is bad, tragedy is wrong, and grief is something we need not endure.

The assumption behind these assumptions, whether expressed or not, however, is that we should have life only in its good forms, never in its bad experiences. While most would never admit to thinking such thoughts, the latent assumption is quite obvious from the expressions of grief that question why bad things happen to good people. Part of the problem, as we saw in the Introduction, is that the Bible itself teaches this assumption. The Book of Job, however, confronts the issue head on. Sometimes bad things happen to good people. Then what? Job concludes that meting out suffering to good (or bad) people is God's prerogative. It is only when Job finally and humbly accepts this divine dictum that the tension in the story resolves and his grief-stricken life is restored to normal.

Philosopher Peter Kreeft notes that while pre-modern societies believed we must conform our will to reality, as Job eventually did, modern societies influenced by Enlightenment intellectualism try to make reality conform to its beliefs. Rather than accept suffering as part of reality, modern people question why we must suffer at all.[5] Ruth Nanda Anshen, writing about evil in humankind, notes that "The idea of progress assured Western man, erroneously, of the inevitable victory of the Good as a positive force in history and in human life, while Evil was considered to be a negative principle eventually to be overcome by God's grace, a fortunate fate, by self-discipline, a righteous life, and now even by technology itself."[6] Frederick Sontag likewise notes that philosophers and theologians have for too long placed their rational assumptions upon God and thus tried to make God fit their preconceived notions of justice and reason. He suggests that modern society has turned the problem of theodicy, the justice of God in the presence of evil, into anthropodicy, the making of God into our own image. In the aftermath of the Holocaust and all of the issues it raised for theology and the justice of God, not to mention our enlightened minds, Sontag says we must begin our questions about God by first of all looking at evil itself. Then we can begin to ask questions about God.[7] From these observations we can see that the modern assumption that bad things are not supposed to happen to good people is misguided positivism, if not an arrogant and presumptuous theology.

Interestingly, this is exactly what Brown learns as he reflects on Mackenzie's suffering. One of the results of tragedy I have witnessed time and again is revealed in Brown's letter. Although "bad things happen to good people," good ultimately comes out of it *if we are willing to faithfully work toward that goal.* Brown admits as much a few lines later in his reflection. "Instead of making us bitter, suffering can make us tender, and help us to focus on others who are going through comparable experiences . . ."[8] This humbling effect is not new. It is found in Peter's advice to his constituents to stop thinking about their own suffering and to consider the suffering of others, not to mention the suffering and death of Jesus Christ (1 Peter 5:9).

This suffering of others is exactly what is behind such God-talk as "Yeah, but there are a lot of others hurting worse than me right now" or "Just remember that somewhere in the world someone else has it a lot worse than you." Such comments accurately reflect biblical teaching concerning suffering. Suffering humbles people and brings communities together as they realize that, indeed they do not have it as bad as others and that, while they are hurting, others need help too.

Surprisingly, while displaying disdain for such trite epithets about God, Brown resorts to similar God-talk when he writes, "everyday is a gift." This proverb is a favorite expression of many trapped in the snares of grief and tragedy, and it becomes an important lesson learned by those who must stay after school in the class of suffering. The fact that it was revealed to Brown during this time of illness shows that much good has already come from the suffering of this innocent little baby. Mackenzie's precious life was not being wasted on the world. Even in her sickness, God was using her small body and precious life to reach out and teach vital, spiritual lessons to others.

Despite the important revelations Brown confronts and the fact that he finds them during the child's sickness, he still refuses to give in to the notion that God is somehow behind little Mackenzie's struggle with life.

> I know that there is one answer that does not tempt: the pious statement that "whatever happens is God's will and we must accept it." It is *not* God's will that you or any one of God's children should suffer or die in infancy. It *is* God's will that you live joyously and fully.[9]

Here we see Sontag's anthropodicy argument fully manifest in Brown's God-talk. Questions arise from this statement. How does Brown know that God wants only joy for our lives? He does not; this is his belief, his personal God-talk myth, being projected upon God. Ironically, however, all throughout this letter to Mackenzie, Brown hints that God is involved in this tragedy.

Brown's God-talk is often used to ward off other God-talk that he is not comfortable with. But with Brown's assertion comes another question: If God is not involved in this situation, then who is? The Devil? Fate? Chance? Are we ready to live in a world where such an impotent God is overruled by evil or a Las Vegas-styled divinity?

Why bother writing about or even worshiping such a God if this deity is so ineffective? This is a clear example of Capps' argument that a difficulty is turned into a problem by the refusal to move toward different questions during a time of crisis. Brown's God-talk clearly opens up more problems than it solves. For example, he writes toward the end of the letter that he, like the psalmist from whom he gets his inspiration, believes in God's power to deliver (Psalm 130:7), yet his God-talk consistently overrules this belief.

We have already encountered Brown's own admission that much comes out of little Mackenzie's struggle with life and death: love, a closer comprehension of God, the embrace of mystery, and the humility of grief. These are many of the gifts that Mackenzie's brief life brought into our world, and even Brown admits that these are good. If we consider second order change, then we need to ask a different, disturbing question: Could this have been the purpose of this tragedy? In a world that, as Brown hints, needs more love and a truer perception of God, could this not have been God's will for her life? We really do not know, but Brown withholds the decision from God and stubbornly, humanistically holds on to the folder of possible rational answers rather than trustingly going with what his very heart has revealed: despite his not understanding the purpose behind this tragedy, little Mackenzie's suffering has brought him and, consequently, his readers, closer to God.

All of Brown's struggle implies that suffering, when viewed from a biblical perspective, is, or eventually can work for, good. Therefore, for the believer who dares to move to a deeper, more mysterious faith, suffering can indeed be perceived as brought about by God. This is not a concept most modern people want to agree with, yet St. Augustine said as much: "Since God is the highest good, He would not allow any evil to exist in His works unless His omnipotence and goodness were such as to bring good even out of evil."[10] The real question is whether we *choose* to believe in this aspect of God's Providence and choose to accept the humbling required of such a choice,[11] or whether we remain convinced only of God's goodness and ours, and, thus, continue to believe that we do not deserve suffering at all.

Throughout Brown's letter to his struggling granddaughter (who survived her brief brush with death), we encounter the very grist of grief. The mysterious is faced head on: "there are things we will never understand" Brown relates. The risk in this precarious life as frail humans is highlighted in Brown's phrase "the vulnerability of love." Brown confronts the injustice of this world once more when he laments "It seems unfair that love . . . should open us up to so much pain."[12] But while God's Love may have opened up Brown to pain, we can also suggest that his limited theological and rational assumptions about God's love and goodness opened most of these theological sores, turning the difficulty of suffering into the problem of God's injustice. This change of thought does not mean that Brown would have hurt any less but that his hurting might have taken a different, more trusting tack had he been more open to what his very God-talk was suggesting: that God was really more involved in this situation than Brown wanted to believe. Those trained in the academic myths of the Enlightenment cling to the belief that they can understand all things by holding on to them. What can't be understood must be brought to the therapist or counselor so that our doubts may be alleviated and our self reassured. This postmodern, pop-psychology spirituality reveals more of a bent toward power than toward trust.[13] To insist that this tragedy is not within the domain of God's will is to limit the power of God and place it in the hands of our frail, human epistemologies. This reveals our desire of divinity (you shall be as gods, knowing both good and evil) that was encountered and fallen to in Genesis 3. In our refusal to see God's will in all things, we reveal our bent toward sin and our desire to replace God with self.[14]

MADELEINE L'ENGLE

The learned pages of the *Christian Century* are not the only places where we can find fertile grounds for our investigation of God-talk. Other writers think the same way that Brown does while revealing a spiritual hunger for the very things they refuse to understand or believe. Madeleine L'Engle's *The Rock That Is Higher* comes very close to accepting the implications of God-talk while still refusing to confront the very Mystery that causes God-talk to arise.[15]

L'Engle's life took a tragic turn on July 28, 1991, when a truck broadsided the car she was riding in. *The Rock That Is Higher* is a lengthy narrative of healing and hope applied through the balm of stories, both biblical and personal. L'Engle describes her healing process both physically and spiritually, yet within these pages we see the same tension we found in Brown's letter to Mackenzie. On the surface of her reflections, we can see that she openly, sometimes vehemently, denies any Divine involvement of God in her accident. Yet, in other portions of her work she introduces the possibility that God works through the very accidents of life. The God-talk she employs paradoxically spans the chasm between these two contradictory beliefs. Caregivers can learn much from a study of L'Engle's thoughts on suffering.

L'Engle writes that she does not believe God created her with one leg longer than the other revealing that she does not believe God is involved in the accidents of life. On the other hand, she affirms early in her work that while she was lying on the operating table she believed, "If God was ready for the curtain to come down on this final act of my life's drama, I was as ready as I was ever going to be." What is the difference between these two beliefs?[16]

L'Engle writes that immediately after the accident she prayed the Jesus prayer, "Lord Jesus Christ have mercy on me." Many pray such prayers in times of duress but what is interesting is what this prayer implies. "Have mercy on me" could ask that God relieve the pain from the pray-er or provide strength in the time of crisis. Or, it may imply that God was somehow involved in the tragedy. While most would no doubt choose the former, a closer look at L'Engle's beliefs reveals that the latter could also be an option.

For example, L'Engle's God-talk demonstrates that she chooses to depict God as the Great Playwright who manipulates our lives like characters in a Broadway show. When she emerges from surgery alive and well, she writes that God still had work for her to do. Such an assertion implies that God was at work in the potentially deadly surgery room and that God allowed the surgery to be successful. Thus, while decrying one form of God-talk that providentially sees God at work in all things, good and bad, L'Engle reveals within her own God-talk a belief that God is very much involved in all things.

As suggested earlier, people paradoxically use God-talk in two ways, and these two patterns often arise in contradiction at different points in our lives. When living within the safety of good health and bounteous life, we often affirm that God does not send misfortune our way. This may be a subconscious and even primitively superstitious way to fend off bad luck. We do not want to believe that God wills ill-fortune so we do not even talk about it. This form of "primitive magic" keeps the spell off of us, if you will.

Caught in the throes of crisis, however, the "rules" have now changed and with that change, the God-talk now changes as well. Now God is very much looked upon as the one who holds our human cards in divine hands. The present crisis has upended our everyday theology and presented us with a potentially dangerous new option: maybe God did this to me. Our God-talk indicates that we instinctively know our life is held in God's apparently capriciously loving hands. If, as L'Engle has written elsewhere, "The Holy Spirit does not hesitate to use any method at hand to make a point to us reluctant creatures" and that there is a "dark side of the divine" then this God-talk implies God is very much involved in our accidents and sufferings.[17]

So we see that there is an inherent tension in God-talk and sometimes this tension is manifest in phrases juxtaposed to each other. This tension is filled with ambiguity and paradox, which is the very stuff of story writing, as L'Engle well knows.[18] And this tension is manifest in L'Engle's own words when she insists that God was not involved in her accident, on the one hand, and that God was very much in control of her destiny on the operating table. If God is in control of one's life on the operating table, then certainly God is in control of one's life in everyday traffic.

Many dodge such tensions by labeling them theological problems that need to be fixed because they do not believe people can live in such ambiguity. Indeed, this is so because the people who seek spiritual and psychological help are often caught between two competing belief systems. Courses in counseling teach that this is a crisis point, a psychological crossroads for the person. In the realm of God-talk, however, we need to understand that ambiguity, paradox, and theological tension are to be expected. Indeed, they may be the very signs of solid faith!

Theologians and philosophers today are slowly correcting the rational ways of the last few hundred years that sought to make straight every bending, confusing theological problem encountered by humans. For example, Peter Kreeft insists that we need to move beyond the truth of reason to the truth of mystery and myth. Professor of Religious Studies Garrett Green argues that we need to allow religion to move back into its real and useful realm of imagination. Old Testament scholar Walter Breuggemann also insists that biblical stories are full of ambiguity and paradox and that any attempt to rid these stories of such tensions does an injustice to them. Theologian Gary Dorrien demonstrates that theology today needs to recapture the imaginative imagery of myth if it is to become useful once more. Myth, imagination, ambiguity, paradox, and tension are the components of good storytelling and, it would seem, good theology. Thus, caregivers need to become more tolerant of such ambiguity in their treatment of God-talk with all of its complexity and ambiguity.[19]

We need the ambiguity of myth and story in our theology because it forces us to work through the complexities of life, helping us to realize that many of these conundrums are simply not solvable. Thus, we need faith to help us move forward in these times of uncertainty. This seems to be the goal of L'Engle as she works through the tension in *The Rock That Is Higher*. She writes that God has a divine purpose and that God is incomprehensible, implying that we will never know the will of God. Indeed, she is comfortable with this since, as she admits, she knows the purpose of ambiguity and that truth has many facets. This opens up the realm of mystery which is an important topic in many of her other spiritual works. In talking about her accident and her long recovery she writes that, "God was coming into this seemingly irrational accident" and that, "nothing, ultimately, is irrational when God has entered into it."[20]

Despite her acknowledgment of the meaning of ambiguity and the purpose of many facets of truth, we see the struggling attempt to rationalize the irrational. For L'Engle, God comes into the irrational accident, and this appearance by God then seems to make sense of the ordeal. That is, God's presence rationalizes the incident. But we have to wonder if L'Engle is really trying to accept an irrational God. Rudolf Otto notes that one of the key characteristics of God is the irrational.[21] When we try to rid the irrational from God's personality, then we have again tied down God into an idol of rationality tooled with the hands of our own reason. If God is truly God, the All in All, then God must be permitted to be both rational and irrational. L'Engle even admits as much when she writes, "If we limit ourselves to the possible and the provable . . . we render ourselves incapable of change and growth." She goes on to write that the more rational we become, the more irrational we turn out to be. Thus, it seems L'Engle is trying to say that God, the irrational author of her life story, is helping her to understand the irrationalities of the plot of her life.[22]

Many look upon God-talk as irrational and fall back upon their human reason to dispel the unreasonable implications of God-talk.

"God is just, therefore God does not harm the good people in life. This must instead be Fate working here." Or, "God is love, therefore God would never deliberately kill (or allow killing) a child with the gun of a crazed killer." Here an "irrational assumption" is dispelled with "rational" God-talk, but the consequences of such reason lead us into the confusing and tedious treatises of theodicy (the justice of God) or logical proofs of how a good God can or cannot allow Evil into the world. As we have noted previously, Capps' pastoral discussion and Kreeft's philosophical work demonstrate that such arguments from reason simply open new theological conundrums and do not solve the issue at all. Rational attempts to explain God in the face of suffering turn into even more irrational explanations of God compared to honest, serious biblical reflections of God's total character.

We can either learn to live with a God who, to us, is irrational, or we can attempt to rationalize our God and turn God into an even deeper irrationality. L'Engle seems to warn against this overdefining of God because she labels such efforts "sin." She writes, ". . . sin is separation from God and one way to separate ourselves from God is to over define God."[23] God-talk used and understood in the proper way tears down this separation caused by overdefinition, making us confront the irrational side of God, deepening our faith and helping us to mature in a greater appreciation for God.

Despite L'Engle's warnings about accepting the rational to the exclusion of the irrational, she unknowingly crosses this line as she writes about her accident. If, as many, including L'Engle believe, God is not the cause of our accidents, then why, as L'Engle writes, does God care about what happens to us after an accident?[24] Why would a God who is out of touch with our lives before and during an accident give a flip about what happens to us and then only *after* the tragedy? If we risk anthropodicy and apply the parental model to God, then we could claim that God, like any decent parent, does not cause accidents to happen to unsuspecting children of the earth but that God, like any interested parent, certainly cares very much about what happens to us. One objection to this line of reasoning is that parents are not omnipotent, omnipresent, and omniscient. Our weekly worship of God, however, certainly betrays this belief in our Creator. Why would we pray to God to be with a person in the hospital or to give a person safe travel if we do not believe that God is ultimately in control of all things? If God is not in control of such things, as certain theodicy and problem of evil arguments make God out to be, then why bother worshiping and praying to such an impotent deity?

Ultimately, L'Engle moves into this land of belief in the ambiguities of life when she admits that her life was beyond the skill of the doctors, implying again that only God determined whether she lived or died. If God was in the hands of the doctors, then could not God also be in the hands of the errant driver who caused her accident? This discrepancy apparently does not bother her, and that is one of the paradoxical facets of God-talk that is so blinding to caregivers. It leads to irrational dichotomies that, like two pillars for the same bridge on opposite sides of the river, simply must stand together. We see L'Engle making and crossing one of these bridges herself through her God-talk. She believes that God was not the cause of her accident, but she trusts that God can very much be the cause of her death or life on the operating table. She believes that God was not involved in her accident but that God was not finished with her life yet. Thus, her life has a purpose after this accident. If this is the case, then why not take the even larger step of faith and trust that God was the cause of her accident to begin with? This is what her God-talk implies.

The problem for L'Engle and others is that she believes God is a God of love. Thus, He would never do such an unloving thing as cause an accident to someone. Yet, the problem is this definition of Divine Love is too narrow here. Peter Kreeft daringly writes, "Perhaps we suffer so inordinately because God loves us . . . perhaps the reason why we are sharing in a suffering we do not understand is because we are the objects of a love we do not understand."[25] We forget that God's love encompasses many other aspects of God's divine temperament. In the stories of the scriptures, L'Engle trustingly quotes from are numerous examples of God's love coming in the form of both retribution and compassion (Ezekiel), of accident and salvation (Joseph), of affliction and comfort (Isaiah 40-55) along with grace and discipline (Paul). God works in both good and bad ways to effect an overall mysterious and heretofore unknown purpose guided by love.

As a writer L'Engle knows truth comes in many forms. One form we need to face is that God's Truth may be the most manifest in the storms of life brought to us by the God of all Creation, which is the assertion Eugene H. Peterson makes in his penetrating study of the Book of Lamentations. Peterson dares to believe that God's Anger can be part of God's Love toward us.[26] The God who causes it to rain upon both the good and the bad (recall that we often ask God to send rain) is also the God responsible for the floods that devastate whole communities and peoples. We do not want to accept this reality, but if we are to wade into the deep ambiguities of faith, as L'Engle invites us to over and over again, then we must learn to ponder the myriad possibilities of the God of both Good and Evil. This then would manifest L'Engle's call to collaborate with the divine purpose which eventually forces us to change and grow,[27] a call to change that sounds much like Capps' second order change.

It is evident, then, that while Madeleine L'Engle believes God would never cause us any harm, she in fact implies that God is in control of our very life. While she writes that God's purposes are mysterious, she works very hard to solve some of this mystery herself by insisting that God is Love and therefore would never hurt one of the beloved creatures. Yet she reveals again and again in the soul of her God-talk that ultimately she believes God is in control of all aspects of our lives and that we need to trust this A-rational Deity's purpose if we are ever to appreciate this life we are given.[28]

MARTIN MARTY

A Cry of Absence was published by Martin E. Marty in 1983 and has proven a faithful companion to sufferers ever since. He leads the reader to ponder grief and its coldest seasons with the help of the Book of Psalms. It was written after the death of Marty's wife as an alternative to "surface consolations or simple assurances" which simply means God-talk. The book, it is said in the preface to the third edition, has helped reshape the reality of the sufferer's soul, a phrase that will come to mean more as we work our way through the maze of God-talk throughout this discussion.[29]

Martin Marty writes for those who are wandering in the winter of the soul. He also writes in response to those who persist in what he terms "summery" Christianity. Marty defines "summery" believers as those who refuse to walk in the cold ways of the sufferer, or those who offer simple similitudes to those in the throes of grief. They are termed "summery" as opposed to "wintry" believers who prefer a more reflective faith. While Marty carefully, pastorally notes throughout his book that there is a time for both types and that different believers exhibit various ways to work through their grief, his dichotomy between the two is still quite pronounced and thus disturbing. He clearly prefers the wintry route and therefore his readers, perhaps uncritically, will follow along with him. Thus, his critique of "summery" believers is potentially misleading and calls for some comment.

I have seen this disparity between those who descend to the depths of despair in their grief and those who lean instead upon proverbial faith. My experience has been that both approaches have their merits and their pitfalls. The pitfalls of both are twofold. On the one hand, simple sayings (Hey, it could be worse, brother; The Lord wills it; God never puts on us more than we can handle.) can be easy ways out for those who refuse to ponder the greater mysteries of the faith.[30] It has been my experience that such shallow people fall to pieces when *their* world suddenly comes apart, and all the bumper sticker faith in the world cannot hold them together. The pitfalls for those who prefer the depths of the soul in which to work out their grief, however, are a wallowing kind of faith that prefers pity more than healing and languishes in the ill-health of sympathy rather than the healing balm of truth.[31]

On the other hand, many are too quick to categorize simplistic God-talk as the drawl of "the country and western" believer, as Marty describes it.[32] Not to mention that such disparaging labels reveal elitist arrogance. As has already been noted, when God-talk phrases are studied and understood within the context in which they are uttered, they prove to be quite deep in a poetically simple way. Likewise, if we probe the context in which they were learned, whether that be through experience, biblical allusions, or great texts of the faith such as hymns, we can discern a ring of truth that, in fact, causes us to ponder their sounds for quite a while. I have witnessed such labels and assessments applied by ministers, and it is appalling that, while we speak of souls as "living human documents" that can be read hermeneutically,[33] we fail to pause long enough to really hear what is being said in, and who is doing the pronouncement of, the God-talk we are confronting.

The fact that "country bumpkins" are not the only ones who offer simplistic proverbs in times of grief is quite obvious just from the previous discussion. Snippets in both Brown's and L'Engle's reflections could very well be labeled "summery." The Introduction discussed how one chaplain even admitted that she thought God-talk was evidence of a simplistic faith until she found herself with sufficient cause—dare we say reason?—to employ it. Summery God-talk is not restricted to those of little faith, and it is wrong to insinuate that only those with crude religious beliefs resort to such language. God-talk often reveals a very deep faith in God that is offered in short truths of poetic proverbs. It may be more true to assert that ignorance is more revealed by those who show complete disdain for God-talk!

Marty illustrates how one dissects and probes a text in order to understand the words of the writer and their implications. His method is informative for our discussion, and I use it in a subsequent chapter. Let us note for now that, if we are to fully understand and appreciate the wisdom and compassion of God-talk, we must treat it as if it were a text, exploring its context, its speaker and the speaker's past as well as the recipient of the God-talk and the recipient's context. It is only then that we can offer an honest and critical pastoral assessment of the veracity or the irresponsibility of the God-talk in question.[34]

Marty worries that some summery believers may unintentionally lead to the ostracization of the one suffering through the magical words of their God-talk. His conclusion is based on history of religion's observations and how "primitive" societies often use these ceremonies to ostracize an individual. The bubbly, summery God-talk may unintentionally ostracize the sufferer to a life of absence instead of the presence of the Deity. Thus, this innocent summery act leads to the killing of the soul of the sufferer.[35] While Marty's conclusion is warranted, I would like to take his observation the other way and demonstrate that this ostracization may indeed be a necessary function in the arena of grief.

Books on suffering note how, as sufferers walk through the various stages of grief, they must endure a death experience of a spiritual kind. The loss of a loved one leads the grieving husband to acknowledge that a part of him has died. The loss of a limb forces the patient to leave behind many tasks that were once performed and enjoyed, not to mention the future dreams that are now lost. This experience feels like death. But more important, tragedy, as many sufferers willingly admit, forces the soul into a deathlike catharsis that only comes from walking through "the valley of the shadow of death," as Psalm 23 perceptively describes it. It is this journey from life-before-tragedy to "death" and then to the "resurrection"-after-tragedy and the perception of God's absence throughout the journey that Marty writes about. Indeed, many psalms speak of the singer's life without God. This is not a new idea; but for those who enter the dark world of grief, it is a new experience altogether.

Those who offer God-talk compassionately, wisely perceive, if only subconsciously, that sufferers need to be cut off from the everyday theologies and forced to walk the lonely path of absence if they are ever to survive the grief process. It is here that we must be reminded of the primitive rites of initiation in which the initiate goes into the wilderness to face the unknown and comes back to the community as a new member of the social order. The similarities between such initiations and the liminal time of grief experienced by a sufferer are too great to be dismissed. Each initiate or sufferer is, in a unique way, touched by the Deity and therefore considered "sacred" and thus too powerful for the "profane" community to be near. Each sufferer experiences a life-death-rebirth "initiation." Each person is considered liminal, marginal, an outcast from the social group until he or she comes out of the process. In essence, each initiate must undergo a spiritual or even physical death experience in which the initiate faces the spirit or deity who changes his or her life. As a part of this experience each person must adhere to strict social/religious rules yet must also find a new spiritual way and meaning for herself or himself. This often includes leaving behind comfortable and naïve social or religious structures in order to become the man or woman the Creator intended the person to be.

Thus, when observed this way, God-talk may not only serve as a catalyst to send the sufferer off to the wilderness in order to find the answers he or she seeks, the God-talk may also symbolically, mythologically prepare the person for the journey. The God-talk serves as a kind of catechism that, when analyzed and accepted (or rejected), leads the person to a deeper understanding of the deity.[36]

Indeed, this is the very path that Marty prefers. In order to grow, Marty advises, one must live in the absence of warmth through the winter of death before one appreciates and grows from the thaw induced by spring sunshine. The metaphors he employs are from the farming world where a seed is dropped into the fallow ground and, after the winter snows, comes to full flower. This is simply the life-death-life cycle of ancient mythology. The initial sting of God-talk offered by a well-wisher may be the very catalyst that forces (plants) one into the grieving process (death as in life underground) that may lead the hesitant one to spiritual growth and psychological healing (new life). While all sufferers need the support of the community, a notion emphasized by Marty in the third edition of his book more than in previous editions, every sufferer knows that eventually one must muster the faith and courage to take the long, lonely walk into the dark recesses of the soul in order to appreciate the light of hope waiting at the other end of grief.

This time of absence and forced ostracism may also be a protection for the God-talker. If we allow ourselves to see this situation in mythological imagery, the one caught up in the fiery and tumultuous storms of trials and tragedy may simply be too much for most people to handle emotionally and spiritually. The anger, the offensive words thrust at God in defiance and grief, the doubt and the disbelief felt and voiced throughout the period may be too much for "young ears" in the faith. Better to ostracize the sufferer from the larger community until it is safe. This does not mean that one must be excluded; it simply acknowledges the obvious—the "profane" friends, family, and community simply do not have the "sacred" theological, professional, emotional, or spiritual tools with which to repair this broken soul. Thus, the most they can offer is a simple "I'll pray for you" as if to wake God up to the plight of their friend or a polite "I'm sorry," which seems to apologize for God's rough treatment of the sufferer. Neither seems sufficient, and both come off as rather ineffective when viewed against the hurricanes of the soul. But deep within their simplicity may be much that sufferers, caught up in the whirlwinds of their own pain, simply cannot see.

A personal example may help to better illuminate this issue. A minister friend lamented to me that he was extremely bothered about the God-talk offered to him when his father died suddenly. As he vented on me and another colleague, I noticed that his very anger was troubling to me and that I did not want to hear his disparaging remarks about God. Because of my heavy pastoral schedule that week, I needed to distance myself from his anger in order to keep from becoming angry myself. To protect my fragile emotions and to keep from saying something inconsiderate, I found myself wanting to deflect my friend's anger and say to him, "You will understand this better someday down the road" which I knew he would and, by his own admission later, he knew as well. In other words, I wanted to use God-talk to offer a nugget that, admittedly would not be of value to him but could be cashed in later after he had worked through the grief and pain of his father's death.

He verified my pastoral hunch when he noted during our conversation how he did not like the God-talk offered to him by friends and well-wishers, especially the phrase "I'm sorry." But he also said that he understood people were just trying to be compassionate. Again, within this tension we see the double-sided effect of God-talk. It is offered in compassion by the talker yet often received in pain by the sufferer. Yet the recipient knows that it is offered in compassion and, after some time, the compassion and the wisdom of the God-talk will become apparent. The pain must simply be endured, because nothing, no matter how well-intended, seems to alleviate the suffering.

This is not to suggest that the suffering person has nothing to offer the caring community. If the caring community has the wherewithal to endure the frustration, anger, and even blasphemy that comes during this liminal time, much can be learned from the suffering person. Still, most, having neither the sacred fortitude nor cognizance of this deficiency, fence themselves off from the grief-stricken person with their God-talk.

The previous scenarios illustrate well that God-talk serves a purpose for both the sufferer and the comforter. For the comforter it is a genuine offering of compassionate wisdom given to the sufferer and it also serves to distance the sufferer from the joyful caring community until the time of grief has passed. This time of absence serves a purpose to the sufferer who must now rethink theologies and even life itself in order to accept the new reality of life lived in the aftermath of his or her losses.

Another point Marty makes is that those who prefer the wintry way of sorting out their grief search for order as does the rest of the world. This search for order is important to all who have entered the Domain of Chaos.[37] While Marty decries those who offer simplistic platitudes and proverbs for those in chaotic times, for those who wish to probe its deeper meanings, this God-talk offers them order for their troubled lives. The wintry soul that finds no boundaries anywhere may be mystified by the phrase "No matter what happens, God is still in control." Yet every sufferer eventually comes to this conclusion, including Marty, who keeps alluding to God's providence as the cause and the reason for the summers and winters of our souls. Indeed, Marty cites Psalm 74:16-17 as support for this view and then says emphatically *"God remains in control."*[38]

This kind of God-talk, while appearing trite on the surface, is really an affirmation of the faith it takes to get one through the maze of grief. In a time of boundaries broken by tempestuous whims of the Creator, the knowledge that God is still somehow in control is a breath of fresh air for those who wish to think through the ramifications of such God-talk. And Marty confirms this assertion by using the psalms, many of which implicate God as the cause for their grief and also praise God for the lessons taught through, and the salvation that could only be brought about by, the tragedy, as he is guided through the disordered world of grief.

Marty ponders the thought, "How, in the midst of a sunny-dispositioned psalm, can one make sense of an absolutely bleak descent into the abyss?" by answering his question a few lines later and throughout his book with the declaration, "And yet one trusts, one praises." Here we see that even "sunny" axioms have a purpose for Marty and have a good effect upon those in the cold of a soul's winter. It seems that, based on this evidence alone, most God-talk is ultimately the wisdom of trust learned in the halls of faith and experience, expressed in various manners of praise.[39]

Thus, we see some ambiguities in Marty's use and interpretation of God-talk. While he prefers solitude, he admits that community is important. While he despises summery talk that seems to distance the sufferer from the community, he extols the long absence-of-community walk he insists most sufferers should make. While he dislikes the summery type of Christianity that seems to belittle those of wintry faith, he often leans toward that style of faith like a plant leans toward the life-giving sun. It would seem that, although he prefers the wintry sort of grief walk that even he admits provides no satisfying answers, he still invokes the joy and the support that comes in the psalmist's affirmation that God is in control of our lives, and thus deserves praise for all things good and bad.

C. S. LEWIS

Martin Marty mentions C. S. Lewis' much respected book, *A Grief Observed*. Thus, we turn to Lewis' observations on grief that ensued after the sudden and tragic death of his newlywed wife. Lewis wades through the river of doubts and fears that come to a believer when tragedy hits suddenly. Grief feels like fear, he writes, and this leads him and the reader to wonder what or who is to be feared. For Lewis, it is two entities: first, the separation from his wife, in relation to which a friend reminded him that Christ also felt separated from God; second, the God who brought about the separation.[40]

Lewis writes, "The real danger is coming to believe such dreadful things about Him. The conclusion I dread is not, 'So, there is no God after all,' but 'So, this is what God's really like.' " Here we see Lewis confronting the limits of his present beliefs of past faith as they clash with the present reality around him. From this point Lewis vacillates between the two poles of Fate (Nature) and God, eventually concluding that even Nature is not as capricious as God. From here Lewis blames God for the tragedy, thus demonstrating that he believes somewhere in his hurting soul that God is indeed behind the tragedy. Like Marty, he too decries the simplistic sort of cheerful statements made by well-wishing Christians. But within this complaint of a man's simplistic God-talk is couched the words, "But in the light of my recent thoughts I am beginning to wonder whether, if one could take that man's line (I can't), there isn't a good deal to say for it."[41]

Lewis' comments help us to see that initial grief reactions to "summery" God-talk belong to the anger portion of the grief cycle. The problem is manifest by Lewis when he writes that his struggle is between holding onto his wife with the arms of memory to the point of creating a myth about her and letting her go, ostensibly to be with God.[42]

Here again we see how God-talk offends to the point of driving someone to confront reality head on. Lewis admits that the phrase "She is with God" has its merits, thus, we can see how a part of him knows the truth of this God-talk phrase. Yet as long as he holds on to her earthly life written indelibly on the pages of his memory, he cannot accept or is not able to accept the meaning and truth of the fact that, for believers, his wife is now in heaven with God. Breaking through this barrier is difficult to do, yet God-talk does so and gives the sufferer the tools to make the transition from our world as we conceive it to God's world as tragedy reveals life the way it really is. In essence, tragedy confronts us with two myths, one being our present human myth and the other the real, divine myth. We must choose which we will live by. Making the transition from human to divine myth, accepting God for who God is, warts and all, is the very abyss through which the sufferer must travel alone in order to make this transition.

Lewis reveals to the reader his struggle with this transitional journey and the validity of the God-talk that forced him to rethink his personal myths. Here we are privy to Lewis' thinking process as he fights between what he wants and what his soul needs. For example, he does not believe in the myth of family reunions in heaven about which our hymnody sings, yet on the previous page he writes, "But my heart and body are crying out, come back, come back." Lewis' God-talk, and the God-talk offered by others is trying to move him beyond this spiritual impasse. Lewis describes his dilemma when he writes, "We *know* it couldn't be like that" but then he goes to say, "and that, just that, is what I cry out for. . . ."[43]

Again and again Lewis fights against the God-talk offered to him while remaining oblivious to the healing balm his own heart is offering him. For example, one friend says that Lewis' wife is happy now and at peace. Lewis cries back, "What makes them so sure of this?" Yet he writes that his wife's last words were, "I am at peace with God." Thus, we witness the veracity of God-talk offered to Lewis.

Part of the grief process and the sufferer's struggle is to make sense of God through tragedy and suffering. Lewis describes this plight in detail as his rational mind tries to make sense of what he eventually comes to see as an irrational God. "Is it rational to believe in a bad God?" he asks.[44] He comes to see God as unreasonable only because our depraved minds cannot correctly conceive of God anyway. Jane Mary Zwerner sums up this mental process by noting "Transfiguration requires some formation which occurs only through suffering.

Hence suffering is not incompatible with the existence of an omniscient, omnipotent, and omnibenevolent divine being."[45] This spiritual process leads Lewis to again acknowledge his fear of God, yet now it appears to be a fear centered around suspense, which is the basis for mystery. This is the beginning of a reverence of God that is based on wisdom, not anxiety, as the biblical writers note when they advise that the fear of the Lord is the beginning of wisdom. The ancient Hasidim of Judaism would say that Lewis is on the verge of knowing the real God: "when you know that God is hidden, then God is hidden no longer."[46]

God-talk understands, embodies and expresses this awe-full, fearful, reverential aspect of the divinity. Couched within its simple aphorisms are experiences and thoughts that are difficult to express, yet they acknowledge that God's sovereignty includes both weal and woe, summer and winter, good and evil. And Lewis' reflection reveals his acknowledgment. As he confronts his feelings with the thoughts that arose during this time of grief, he realizes that his prior faith has been just imagination. He then sees God in a new way, as a surgeon. This new myth suggests to him that God must often cut with a knife in order to produce healing. He then offers a profundity that is very helpful to those caught in the confusing whirls of grief: a desperate need for God may in fact cloud a person's hearing of God.[47]

Lewis begins to put together his new post-tragedy myth by leaving the notion that God is a sadist who takes away our pleasures just when we were beginning to enjoy them. He proceeds to the new concept that God saw that Lewis' marriage had been perfected and that it was now time to move on to something else. Here we see God-talk as well in the genre of Lewis' new myth. God, according to Lewis, took his wife from him when the marriage reached a perfect state, thus indicating to him it was now time to move to another page in his life. This notion strikes many, including Lewis before this tragedy, as cruel. What kind of God would do this? But this is the new myth that Lewis' grief leads him to write (or accept). From here Lewis moves into even more claims about God that demonstrate he is in the realm of a new, developing myth, one that helps him to better comprehend, and thus live, to the full the life God has given him after this tragedy.[48]

With the help of Lewis, we see how the grief process leads one to rewrite the myths that guide and inform our lives. The process is initiated by the God-talk that hints of such myths to a sufferer. Indeed, the God-talk seems to spur the sufferer to confront inadequate myths and look for new ones that better explain or support reality. The process leads to anger and deep questions about God and the purpose of life. Yet the God-talk eventually leads to an acceptance (or rejection) of the new myth that better describes the real God rather than the one we have concocted in our personal, pretragedy mythologies.

RABBI HAROLD S. KUSHNER

Kushner's best-selling book, *When Bad Things Happen to Good People,* has comforted sufferers since 1981.[49] Many have turned to its pages for answers to questions that seem to elude even the best theologians. The book is a personal and passionate exploration of the author's grief and ensuing questions of faith after the loss of his son who fought a fourteen-year battle with progeria, a rapid-aging disease.

Kushner writes that, upon hearing the diagnosis, he immediately asked the questions that all of us would ask. "Why is this happening to me? I have tried to live a good life. If God was 'minimally fair' let alone loving and forgiving, how could He do this to me?"[50] His questions and their assumptions call for some comment.

Here we see what I call the sin of presumptuousness, the very sin of which the otherwise righteous Job was guilty. This modern belief insists that I deserve only good to happen to me. Behind this belief is the dubious implication that I am good, therefore, I deserve good. Kushner reveals this inclination when he candidly admits that he thought this kind of tragedy only happened to bad people.[51]

Kushner's overall dilemma rests in two issues. First, his own perceptions of God cloud his ability to fully wrestle with the God he is experiencing. We see no attempt to explore competing interpretations of God as we saw with C. S. Lewis. Instead, Kushner, like the Jacob of old, is forcing God to live according to his way of thinking, not according to divine will. Rabbi Kushner insists that God play within the ropes of fairness and justice while wielding all-wise and all-powerful blows, yet these two positions promote a theological tension throughout Kushner's writing that he does not or will not see. The tension exists because he wants to limit God's omnipotence by keeping God confined within the walls of fairness. Part of this tension rests also in his insistence in the "supreme value of an individual's life" and the absolute belief that God is ultimately good. But his assertions raise questions. Can we as humans really know what God's "good" is all about? Do we dare to think we know what this good is? Other questions arise from his comments as well. Does the supremacy of a person's life override God's omnipotence? If so, isn't this a bit self-centered, a trait that has plagued our interpretations of God in this modern generation? If something is all-powerful, then this entity is not restricted by the rules of fairness and justice.[52]

Then there is the deeply philosophical question that emerges from these points: Would we even have God's goodness if it were not for evil? In other words, even though we do not want to admit it, there may be a reason within God's ultimately good plan for evil (tragedy, corruption, tests, suffering, etc.) if for no other reason than that such problems teach us to depend on God, not ourselves and our rational theologies, to help us through the suffering.[53]

Throughout his work Kushner stubbornly refuses to turn himself loose from his positivistic beliefs in the primacy of humanity, the rule of justice that permeates our world and the goodness of God. It is this belief in the positive rational theology of our modern, Enlightenment society which colors and impedes Kushner's efforts to find an acceptable answer to his spiritual dilemma.[54]

Second, Kushner writes to cure the "bewilderment and the anguish" of those who must comfort their afflicted family caught in the winds of life's storms. But can we really cure such ailments of the soul? We have seen that this time of tragedy is really a time of wandering through the wilderness of the soul, as depicted in Marty's work. There is less a cure to be found than a reworking of personal theologies to be done. Kushner betrays the modern, therapeutic mentality that seems bent on relieving suffering altogether rather than dealing with it and growing from it.[55]

He begins his spiritual quest through the halls of tragic darkness by exploring the question, "Why do bad things happen to good people?" While the authors discussed previously at least danced politely with some of the very answers they initially refused to accept, Kushner adamantly refuses to dance with anything that does not fit his theological agenda or his divine constraints. One of the answers he refuses to accept is that people suffer at the hands of God because they have done something wrong, thus they deserve such suffering. He says, "it teaches people to blame themselves. It creates guilt even where there is no basis for guilt." Again his assumption that God is just prejudices his theology. If God is all-powerful, as Kushner initially insists, then God can do whatever to whomever whenever, just or unjust as it may seem to us. Thus, affliction may indeed come to somebody whether he or she deserves it or not. This was certainly Job's dilemma, and we will see in a later chapter that, according to the ancient mythology of the Hebrew people, this unjust notion is biblically not to mention mythically correct.[56]

We find another tension point for Kushner when he confronts the typical answer to tragedy that "everything has a purpose." He recoils against this by saying such an answer comes from people who believe that "God is a loving parent who controls what happens to us." Although Kushner likewise believes God is a loving parent, he apparently forgets this as he denies the "everything-has-a-purpose" side of God-talk. Such excuses, he notes, defend God and leave the sufferer in limbo. Later, however, Kushner denies his own words when he writes that we can learn through the tragedies around us. If we can learn through the tragedies around us, might this then be the very reason for the tragedies?[57]

Even though he derides those who defend God, he is guilty of doing just that when he suggests that nature, not God, kills in the violence of hurricanes, tornadoes, and earthquakes.[58] This begs the question, Did not God create such natural things as the Red Sea incident, the storm, and the whale that imperiled Jonah, and the three-year cycle of drought in Elijah's time? To put this in a modern perspective, farmers in my area have prayed for rain during the droughts in the late 1990s to bust the devastating dry season. When Hurricane Floyd devastated the lower one-third of North Carolina in 1999, many wondered if their prayers for rain were the cause of the hurricane. If we believe that God controls nature (why else would we pray for rain to end a drought?) then, logically and faithfully speaking, would not God be responsible for the drought-ending hurricane? If we say that God has no control over nature, then are we ready to accept the fatalistic concepts that ensue?

Those who defend God may be guilty of faulty theology, but they may also be speaking from a deep personal reflection or relating words of wisdom they heard from someone who has suffered in the past. Such God-talk comes from an extensive vocabulary of personal and archetypal experience which realizes that eventually, should the sufferer exhibit a healthy inclination to heal from this experience, something good, a teachable moment, personal growth, or even a restructured and more relevant theology will arise from the tragedy. This is what happened to Job and, as we found in the previous accounts of other sufferers, they too have benefitted from their tragedies.

Kushner halfheartedly states, "Maybe God does not cause our suffering. Maybe it happens for some reason other than the will of God."[59] Citing Psalm 121:1-2, he decides that God does not do such things yet plenty of other psalms, not to mention other Old Testament passages, indicate that God does indeed afflict us. Perhaps even more important, however, is the theological dilemma Kushner's suggested solution raises: Why believe in a God who is so out of touch with creation and who is that impotent concerning the everyday affairs of our lives?

Kushner promotes a humanistic nihilism when he states that sometimes there simply is no reason for the tragedies in life that befall us. Yet he contradicts himself in many ways. For example, he writes that God has given us a "wonderful, precise, orderly world."[60] If God has given us such an orderly world then this implies that there is a reason for all the orderly disorder that permeates this world. Yet Kushner denies that such a reason exists at all. Ironically, Kushner seems to be looking for a reason when he contradicts himself again by implying throughout his work that death has a reason even if we cannot define it. He does not probe this reason, possibly because to do so would violate his previous conclusion that God does not do harm to the creatures on earth. Yet we must ask this question: If there is a reason for death, then might there also be a reason for suffering, tragedy, trials, and tribulations that bring us near to, if not all the way through, death's door?

If, as he insists, God does not send us tragedy in order to teach us a lesson, then why does Kushner admit in a discussion of the fall of Adam and Eve that we can learn from this experience? If we believe in God's omnipotence and Providence, then is it that much of a stretch to say that God teaches us through tragedy?

Perhaps Kushner's most perplexing conclusion comes in his discussion of the Holocaust. He refuses to believe that God was in any way involved in the Holocaust, and he ties this in with his discussion on suffering. "To try to explain the Holocaust, or any suffering, as God's will is to side with the executioner rather than with his victim, and to claim that God does the same."[61]

Again we see Kushner's refusal to leave behind his defense of God as just and good. This comes despite the Hebrew scriptures that plainly describe God as one who sends in Assyrians, Babylonians, Satan, a lying spirit, and myriad other afflictions to teach, punish, or just mystify the hapless creatures of Creation. Such a belief as espoused by Kushner leaves God only to stand helpless alongside the sufferer while (super?) humans defy all notions of justice and goodness and slaughter millions of innocent people. This discomforting theology is unwittingly summed up nicely by Kushner in the title to Chapter 7: "God Can't Do Everything, But He Can Do Some Important Things."

How did God become so impotent? Kushner unwittingly blames himself when he writes in the final chapter, "I believe in God. But I do not believe the same things about Him that I did years ago . . . I recognize His limitations. He is limited in what He can do by the laws of nature and by the evolution of human nature and moral freedom." Why do we continue to believe in this way? Kushner reveals the answer in a sentence that could be summarized as theological laziness: "I can worship a God who hates suffering but cannot eliminate it, more easily than I can worship a God who chooses to make children suffer and die, for whatever exalted reason."[62]

It is this philosophical and theological laziness that interferes with the proper interpretation, appreciation, and use of God-talk. The implications of God-talk demand that we do more than summarily toss it to the side because it does not fit our theological fancy. A lazy theology diminishes God to the roll of sidekick to the gods of Nature, Chance, Fate, or Human Reason. Consequently, this leaves the sufferer facing chaos without any help in sight.[63] In Capps' pastoral care terms, Kushner has created problems out of dilemmas.

We can see the opposite of such theological narrow-mindedness in the daring thoughts of Holocaust survivor Elie Weisel who has wrestled with these paradoxical depictions of God like few others. He notes that we cannot get rid of the paradoxes but that we must instead learn to live with them. One of these paradoxes is that both hope and despair live within religion. Since we cannot get rid of them, the testing of faith may be the only way for us to understand the necessity of paradox in our faith lives. He goes on to note that a depiction of God as indifferent, which Kushner's impotent and helpless God certainly is, confronts us with a dangerous deity. Weisel instead prefers to deal with the implications of the unjust God. He writes that an indifferent God is incapable of making the Creation. He also writes that "God is one; He is everywhere. And if He is everywhere, then he is in evil and injustice too, and also in the supreme evil: death."[64]

From this discussion we see that God-talk is a very important catalyst in the grief process. While we may initially deny God's involvement in our crisis, our own God-talk actually reinforces the very idea we try to evade. Thus, our God-talk reveals a deep-seated longing for acceptance of a side of the Deity we normally try to ignore. God-talk causes us to confront our current, comfortable theologies and to question previous theological assumptions. It can move us through the valley of the shadow of death. If we choose, we can learn from it and begin to see a new and awe-full side of God that inspires trust and the development of a myth that is more realistic about the true God. This God, according to our God-talk, is both irrational and rational, an all-encompassing Creator of both good and evil.

Chapter 2

Theology, Myth, and Imagination in God-Talk

In the previous chapter we have seen how God-talk is often misinterpreted. Much of the problem, as Daniel Liderbach explains, is that theologians and philosophers have for too long focused on the rational solution of suffering to the detriment of the imaginative explanation or interpretation of suffering.[1] Since God-talk is often misinterpreted by caregivers in pastoral situations and since pastoral caregivers are influenced by philosophical theologians, we need to explore this problem from the viewpoint of theology. Once in the realm of theology we can then move into recent discussions of theology and its relation to myth and imagination. With these arguments in place, we can then proceed to break down God-talk into the various genres we discussed in the Introduction.

JOHN MACQUARRIE'S GOD-TALK

In 1967 theologian John Macquarrie published *God-Talk: An Examination of the Language and the Logic of Theology.* He begins by noting that "theology" is equivalent to "God-talk." Theology is simply a way of talking about God. From this we can assume that we can break apart, examine, and put back together the God-talk we encounter in everyday pastoral experiences much like we would critique, examine, and argue about theological issues. Once stated this way, however, we cannot assume that our analysis of God-talk should follow the academic methodologies of logic and reason. Passionate convictions, Macquarrie explains, reveal deeper issues at stake and these issues are often revealed in the way we talk about God, that is, in theology. Thus, we must move beyond academic examinations and explanations of God-talk if we are to understand God-talk in its pastoral setting.[2]

The context from which God-talk arises is important for Macquarrie and also for caregivers. Macquarrie suggests that we look in the context of the whole theology as presented to us in a pastoral situation. This includes not only the person but also such parameters as the person's life, the present moment, the people around the sufferer, and the situation at hand. This comes as no surprise to pastoral caregivers but, as Howard W. Stone observes, sometimes in the moment of grief even trained pastoral caregivers forget to look at the whole context and instead retreat to familiar theologies.[3] This point was certainly borne out in the previous chapter.

To examine the whole theological context, Macquarrie employs a model that is beneficial for caregivers. He begins by reminding us that we focus too much on language and not enough on the discourse of which the language is a part. Language implies discourse. Unfortunately, theologians and those in biblical studies have for too long focused only on technical terms and not on narrative and discourse. Citing the work of James Barr, Macquarrie argues that we need to move beyond words, terms, and theological buzzwords (i.e., love, goodness, theodicy), and instead look at the discourse such words and terms are inviting.[4]

Macquarrie sees four components in the discourse of God-talk. First, there is the person voicing God-talk. Next, there is the God-talk that is spoken. Then, there is the person spoken to, and finally, there is the subject matter of the larger "discourse situation." This model is no stranger to pastoral caregivers, but in my experience, and as Stone warns, we tend to ignore the subject matter in the larger discourse. Macquarrie's model helps us to see how this subject matter is "deflected" from us in the pastoral conversation, thus leaving out a major portion of the discourse (see Figure 2.1).

The model shows in graphic form how we can follow the line of discourse from the speaker to the listener and focus on what is being said while not fully following what is being implied in the discourse situation. Note that if, in our pastoral work, we cut off or ignore the portion of the graphic "Subject Matter," we strike out as much as two-thirds of the total discourse pie. Macquarrie advises, "When something is said

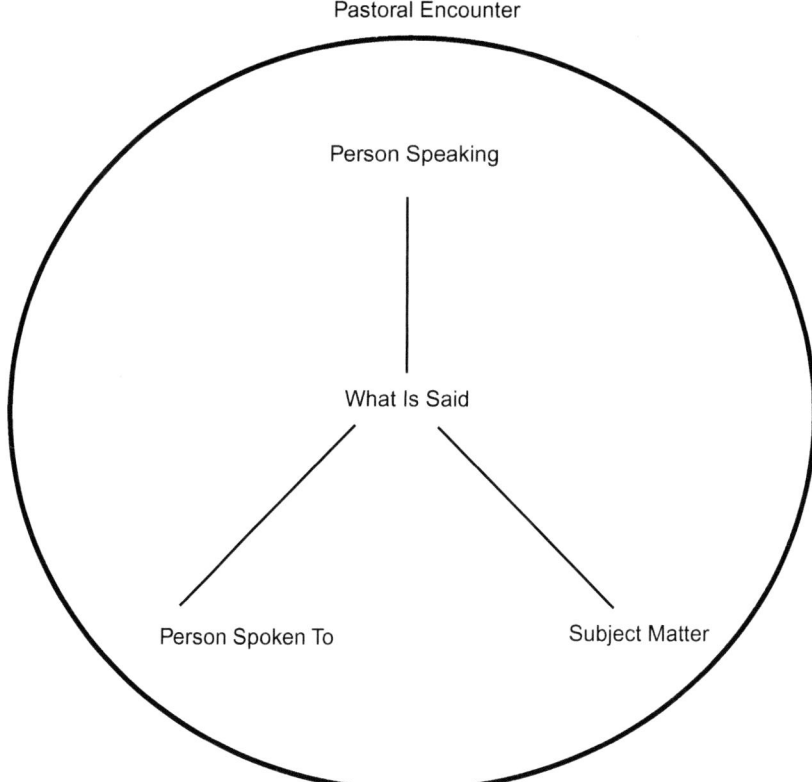

FIGURE 2.1. Diagram Adapted from John Macquarrie's *God-Talk,* p. 65

in a given situation, the language might imply something more, or something different than was explicitly intended by the speaker."[5]

What is this "discourse"? Macquarrie notes that discourse is the personal situation or the personal dimension. If we dismiss the God-talk from this person, we in effect dismiss the personal dimension of both the God-talk and the speaker. We must be aware of the many dynamics in the discourse situation. These include a person's history, his or her story, and the type of imagery used in the discourse such as myth, paradox, fantasy, fighting words, biblical images, etc.[6] I have already suggested that we need to look at God-talk in the genres of myth, story, tragedy prayer, apocalyptic, and wisdom. The pastoral caregiver must not only be aware of *what* is being said, in the discourse situation but also *how* it is being said, and thus the implications of what is being said. There is a big difference in the way theology is discussed and the way a story is revealed. Myth can be very subtle, or it can be quite obvious. Instead, we might miss the particulars of tragedy by focusing on only the suffering and grief of the client. We may retreat from violent outbursts such as "Oh my God!" or "God will get you yet, buddy!" unless we have the pastoral forethought to realize that these are not just emotional ejaculations but a prayer and an apocalyptic utterance. Of course, we do not have the time to pause and think about what genre of God-talk the sufferer is employing in the heat of the emergency waiting room which is why it is all the more important to do our homework before arriving in this situation. We must know instinctually what type of language is spoken to us in the pastoral context and what the dynamics of that language entails.

For example, when we hear someone cry out, "Why is God doing this to me?" we may think the person is looking for answers to the current crisis. Thus, we may try to answer with a response based on a learned argument from theodicy while never once considering that what we have just heard is not a request for an advanced course in the problem of evil but was instead a lament that, frankly, only God can answer. *Intent is just as important as content.*

Here is where Macquarrie's suggestion of intuition comes into play. Intuition must roam into the experiences of theological language. Are faith, grace, creaturely feeling, a sense of the holy, commitment, or adoration present in the God-talk? In the above example, the cry of "Why?" may be a genuine prayer or outburst of grief from an otherwise adoring, trusting, faithful servant. If this is so, it does not need an answer from a simple mortal. On the other hand, it may very well be an irate sufferer, demanding an answer from the only available representative of an absent God. Learning to trust our intuition is the key to understanding the God-talk spoken in pastoral situations.[7]

I have argued previously that God-talk and its peculiar and quite suggestive theology only arises in the time of suffering. Macquarrie verifies this observation when he notes that the time of *angst*, that is, the time of anxiety that eventually comes our way in life, is especially ripe for discourse as well as intuition. He defines *angst* as "the sense of the precariousness of an existence that at any time may cease to exist."[8] This is an excellent pastoral description of a tragic moment and the concomitant crisis of theology it brings with it. Faced with the sudden realization of our finitude in times of tragedy, questions that lay buried in everyday experiences suddenly rise to the surface. Our God-talk gives voice to these questions. Our language becomes more emotive, and, based on Macquarrie's previous suggestions, should not be dismissed just because it is irrational. Emotive language, Macquarrie argues, may lack the precision that academics are so accustomed to—it is not logical, rational, reasonable—but it is still true in the greater sense of Truth.[9]

In essence, what we are faced with in the God-talk voiced in the discourse situation of the crisis is the very real theology of the person. This was demonstrated quite well in the previous chapter where we discovered the paradoxical phenomenon that sufferers often disparage some God-talk while using their own God-talk that made the same implications they disparaged. And this is why it is so important for the caregiver to understand God-talk and all its implications. Macquarrie believes that God-talk does not have to be clear for it to bear truth. He even goes so far as to say that this language may be "logically odd."[10] This notion of illogical or even disparate language and logic was encountered in our discussion of Capps' second order change and also in philosopher Peter Kreeft's discussion of suffering. This terminology—"logically odd"—leaves us with a somewhat confused position concerning this Truth. If we change the terminology, we will find another way to describe it. This is what Liderbach does when he describes such language as "imaginative myth."[11] Thus, it appears that in the discourse of suffering, we need a nonrational language that gives voice to what the sufferer is really feeling and experiencing. This can be done, Macquarrie notes, if professionally trained caregivers will dare to drop the Enlightenment-influenced, logical positivism theology and philosophy we employ to interpret sufferers' God-talk and instead seek meaning in the way God-talk is used. It will be argued below that this can be done by leaving the narrow courts of reason for the broader playing field of imagination.

Macquarrie tries to make a distinction between religious language—praying, praising, blessing, cursing, and other types of religious utterance—and theological language, but his categorical boundary becomes fuzzy when he notes that there is a "close connection between theology and the living faith." Perhaps we should see these two types of language as two sides of the same coin of faith. Indeed, Macquarrie follows this conclusion by suggesting that people's reflections upon their religious language and the rituals that foster such reflection become and reinforce their God-talk. The key, then, is this time of reflection.[12]

Reflection is what lies behind the theology of God-talk in my experience. I have suggested that the biblical writers reflected on their experiences with God and then wrote them down with the vision of hindsight. These writings were chosen later as scripture because they reflected a pervading Truth that echoed the collective experiences of others. This transcendent Truth becomes scripture because it meets the needs of all generations, not just that of the writers. It addresses religious, spiritual, and psychological concerns over time. This is the essence of scripture. These ancient reflections were passed on because they made sense and they worked.

Within these reflections we often see changes in theology. I have mentioned how many biblical writers believed in the theology of "Do good and God will bless; Do bad and God will curse." The Book of Job debunks this as myth and offers a new interpretation of God, one that says God will punish whomever God wants to punish for whatever reason, just or unjust. When Ezekiel was called to comfort his deported flock in Babylon, he changed their theological outlook by calling into question the old belief that God would mete out to the third and fourth generations the punishment for the sins of the first generation. Instead, he prophesied that God would punish individuals for their sins. These are just two examples of how reflection during the time of crisis led to changed theologies and therefore new myths about God. In essence, the God-talk was changed to make sense of the immediate crisis.

Along with this, I have noticed that those who have experienced suffering and have survived with their faith intact seem to "know" something that others do not. Whether this comes from a period of intense retrospection or from some type of revealed gnosis is unclear. An example of such religious experience can be found in patients who have survived heart attacks. It is well known in pastoral circles that these people change spiritually. Indeed, families are advised by medical staff to look out for psycho/religious changes in their loved one after such an experience. Other examples might be that of older people who pass on their God-talk wisdom to others and seasoned pastors who have observed many survivors and their strong faith. Young people, who have not had enough experience with suffering to fully understand the ramifications of their God-talk will often say, "Well, *they say* God won't put on you anymore than you can bear," or, "*I've always heard it said* that there is a reason for these things if you are willing to wait for the answer." Such God-talk implies they have heard these aphorisms from others but have not personally experienced the truth of this God-talk. When the caregiver takes the time to look behind the reflection of the God-talk, then the real theology and implications of the God-talk can be fully understood.

The process of reflection is manifest in two ways. It comes from others, thus the God-talk is laden with reflective truth that, should we take the time to ponder it, reveals much about the person and the God-image in that person's theology.[13] The reflection may also come later, either by the person or through the probes of the caregiver. "What does it mean to say that God took Uncle Harry? Do you really believe God creates storms to change our lives? On what do you base this?"

Wayne E. Oates notes that this process of reflection often reveals a discernible pattern that, in the eyes of faith, suggests God is indeed the cause and the comfort of the present crisis. Such a reflective process removes the tragedy from the secular gods of Luck and Chance and places them into the providential hands of God. Oates suggests that a biblical example of such a process may be found in the story of Joseph (Genesis 37-50) where the hapless Joseph understands that, although others meant to do him harm, God meant it for good. This story is an excellent example of how the Wisdom literature teaches us to reflect upon the events of life to see the greater purpose, that is, the Way of God.[14] Howard W. Stone likewise advises pastoral caregivers to take up the process of reflection as they contemplate the difficult topic of suffering.[15]

As the reflective process takes over in the sufferer, the God-talk may assume a mythical form. This should not surprise us. Macquarrie notes that "primitive" theology often came in mythical form. This type of God-talk does not conform to our rational pastoral approaches, and, thus, may throw us off base as we try to interpret God-talk in the pastoral encounter. When our culture left the primitive, mythical mode of religious thinking, Macquarrie argues, our society was faced with a difficulty: how do we talk about the gods? Macquarrie suggests that we need to stretch our theological language to describe our complex deity. Citing Psalm 78:2, he points out that we need to use parable, riddle, simile, in order to better describe God. He then goes on to suggest that we use analogy, paradox, metaphor, and symbolism.[16]

These categories suggest literature, not theology, and Liderbach notes that the best explanations of suffering have come not from theologians and philosophers but from the poets, artists, and writers who have imaginatively examined the tragedies of life. Such artists incorporate the categories of paradox, ambiguity, metaphor, and mystery, as well as others, into their works. Literary categories, however, may suggest "fiction" to many caregivers with the implication that nontruths permeate God-talk. Macquarrie understands this fear of the illogical and suggests that we need to see this type of language as using "other logics" rather than labeling it as illogical.[17]

An artistic, poetic interpretation of tragedy, as we will see in a later chapter on the genre of tragedy, opens up for us a new dimension of the deity in faith development. Macquarrie eventually suggests that myth is "the matrix out of which the refinements of religious language, including theological language itself, have arisen." He laments that, with "the decline of myth as an intelligible form of discourse, religious faith too has tended to decline." He notes that while modern society has downgraded myth, thus suggesting that we only believe in verifiable scientific proofs, we have instead replaced it with our own myths such as progress, nationalism, and scientism.[18]

THE EXCLUSION OF MYTH IN THEOLOGY

This tendency to delegate myth to the back seat of theological pastoral care is puzzling when the early church resorted to myth to make sense of the suffering, death, and resurrection of Jesus.[19] The history of theology, however, reveals that theologians have neglected and even downplayed myth in their efforts to achieve scientific proof and academic approval of religious arguments. Gary Dorrien's investigation of this matter proves that, while theologians in the past several centuries have tried to rid their craft of myth, this enigmatic literary category still stubbornly insists on being heard.[20]

Dorrien asks perceptively, What kind of Christian belief is possible with a desacralized world? He notes that theological liberalism, in its desire to be progressive and modern, transcends myth. When neo-orthodoxy responded to this crisis, the disparity of theologies only added to the problem while addressing the category of myth. Liberation and postmodern theologies have done no better. In their own form of paradoxical God-talk, Dorrien demonstrates that theologians have shown unwittingly the importance of myth for believers throughout their works that have at the same time sought summarily and ironically to rid doctrine of myth altogether.

For example, in summarizing Schleiermacher's theological method, Dorrien writes:

> If the heart of religion is in religious experience rather than any doctrinal or scientific account of religion, it follows that doctrinal and scientific forms of discourse are severely limited in their capacity to grasp, judge, or express religious truth. Poetic and rhetorical modes of language are much better suited to express the truths of religious experience, even though these forms of discourse inevitably employ language about God's "will" and historical "actions" that are mythical.[21]

Here we see another example of the theologian's reluctance to make judgments about God's will and place in the history of humans, yet we have seen in our examples of God-talk that this is exactly what God-talk does. God-talk tries to find both God's will and, therefore, some sense of the present tragedy that is very much historical in the minds of the sufferers. Liderbach appears to offer a response to this missing link in our theological language when he writes, "The foundation for living in the spirit is that God is present absolutely everywhere, in every possible human experience [with the implication that] there is meaning in the suffering of every person. That meaning is that the victim responds to the summons of the spirit within the enigmatic and forbidding problem of suffering." In a similar and practical observation, Oscar Cullmann, writing about New Testament prayer, reminds us that mere mortals do not know what to say to God in prayer in times of crisis. Thus, God's Spirit tells them what to speak. His point is that, if God is somehow involved in the present tragedy, then God, through the Spirit, the Comforter, is the only one who can correctly say through us what needs to be said concerning the crisis. Thus, God is very much with us in the crisis, because God lives within us in the Spirit. This helps us to understand better what Liderbach goes on to argue. God is found within the suffering, and thus a myth is crafted by the sufferer to help understand this historical experience.[22]

Part of the problem, Dorrien writes, is that as culture progressed and as the Enlightenment influenced the interpretation of religion, we "sought to erase the conflicts between religion and science by making religion scientific. . . . Words such as process, evolution, and progress functioned as virtual God-terms in the vocabulary of theological modernism."[23] Here we see two problems. First, we presume that science and religion are an either/or problem. Instead, we need to see them as but two of various ways to interpret daily phenomena, as world religions expert Huston Smith has so eloquently observed. Second, we also see a shift from the pre-modern mythical terminology to a modern industrial vocabulary. Thus religious experiences are denoted as backward, primitive, and even fictional when compared to the scientific, progressive academic truth our modern day systems encourage. As Christianity took over such systems to voice its theology, Dorrien observes that "it has sacrificed some important aspects of the religious character of its biblical faith."[24]

Dorrien notes that, although liberal theology deemed itself scientific, it was, in effect, highly subjective. Thus we see that the subjective interpretations of religious experience were simply replaced with other subjective interpretations. Neoorthodoxy, led by Karl Barth, tried to disclose this mistake by reemphasizing myth. Barth tried to put the "mysterious" back into the theological conversations. But this approach led to the total emphasis upon myth at the expense of history which led to cries of fiction versus history. This led to Bultmann's demythologizing methodology which sought to get beyond the myths of the early church to the "real Jesus," which seemed to many to sacrifice myth for historical verification. These two methods clashed in an either/or battle on the theological war lines.

The 'neoorthodox' movement thus produced highly developed theological systems that claimed that Christianity contains no myth, other theologies that claimed that Christianity is unfortunately loaded with mythical teaching, and various mediating theologies that sought to minimize the problem of myth in Christianity.[25]

Tillich, Dorrien continues, wisely noting that myth brings together scientific and religious elements, contended that modern theologians were presented with the task of translating the religious truth in biblical and early Christian myth into a myth that modern people could understand. However, as Gilkey later warned, the problem here is that we use human experiences to interpret divine reality, thus risking reducing the complex God to the demarcations of this world. This process, Dorrien concludes, exalts a humanistic interpretation of life that seems opposite to God. Gilkey, Dorrien notes, correctly argued that we needed mythical religious language to unite analogy, revelation, and paradox into a single God-language.[26]

This, according to Liderbach and Gerkin, is exactly what happens when sufferers explain their crises in mythical terms. Literary categories such as analogy are used imaginatively to interpret the paradoxical revelation that stems directly from the spiritual experience in suffering. Thus, God-talk would seem to be a theological language that does what Gilkey asks.[27]

While Gilkey was on the mark in his determination that our secular world needed religious myth to interpret its everyday life, Dorrien points out that Gilkey made the mistake of using the language of sociology and psychology as the community in which these myths were to be created. Here we see how Gilkey was both right and wrong. He was correct in suggesting that people use the terminology of their community in which to interpret tragedies. Yet, he left the vocabulary of the faith community—the scriptures—for another vocabulary altogether in which to describe its encounters with God, a move which led to the religion of psychology and the resulting cult of self-worship and the new sins of victimization. In essence, Dorrien writes, Gilkey's new myth still clung to the notion of God's Providence as limited by the freedom of humanity.[28]

The ensuing liberation and post-modern theologies did no better. Dorrien's discussion of recent theologies makes it plain that liberation and post-modern theologians saw themselves as myth-makers trying to replace older, patriarchal myths with newer, more appropriate myths. Thus, we see again that the theological enterprise is simply myth-making and re-mythologization. Dorrien then makes a most appropriate assertion:

> If Tillich, Niebuhr, Gilkey, McFague, and the Jungians are right that myth is intrinsic to theology, it follows that theologians should use mythical language normatively in as creative and compelling a manner as possible. If, on the other hand, theological liberalism and its spiritual descendants are right that theology can and must transcend myth if it wants to make credible cognitive claims, then a thoroughgoing program of demythologization is necessary for theology and faith.[29]

Thus, we are back to the either/or dichotomy as to whether myth has a normative role in theology or not. The issue seems to be the interpretation of God's transcendence, which is certainly the main thrust in interpreting suffering. Dorrien concludes, "If divine transcendence is understood as God's creative power to overcome nonbeing, and if this conception is supported by some appeal to an experience of God as the power or ultimate ground of being, then myth becomes indispensable to theology."[30]

It is not clear what or who Dorrien means by "nonbeing," but it appears to mean that God uses divine transcendence to enter the physical world of (human) being. When God does this, humans are affected in some way, either for good or ill, and thus need some system in which to describe or explain this transcendence. The only system available that adequately provides for such explanations of these experiences is myth. Thus, theology, in its desire to put God into words, must employ myth.

Interestingly, if we recall the New Testament Book of John, we already have a prime example of God living in a Word that can only be appropriately described religiously as myth: Jesus Christ. Thus, we are back to a biblical example of how God speaks to us in words that can be termed myth and how those relating the manner in which God has spoken to them also resort to myth.[31]

MYTH AND THE RELIGIOUS IMAGINATION

The problem of Dorrien's and Liderbach's criticism is that neither tells us how to employ an imaginative, mythical approach to our experiences, especially in the realm of theology which is the language of ministry. Fortunately, theologian Garrett Green has made some suggestions as to how to begin incorporating imagination and thus myth, back into the theological discussion. In his *Imagining God,* he notes that both sides of the debate insist that religion is an imaginative process.[32] Thus he suggests we need to incorporate imaginative qualities in our theological assessments of God and learn to accept these as correct.

Green states that the Bible, for Christians, is *the* paradigm for imaginative interpretations of God's dealings with human kind and with creation. Green reminds us that the Bible is authoritative for Christians. It is used by the Christian community for interpreting their lives. "As such," says Green, "scripture is the means by which individual and group identity is formed and reformed." He points out further that the Bible as paradigm for the faith community also has within it many differing paradigms that, working together, collectively paint a portrait of the God who encounters humans. If we recall Gilkey's sociological and psychological model of community, we note that Green has brought us back to the faith glue of the Christian community. The Bible is used as the paradigm to interpret the good and bad, the weal and woe of life. And within its pages we find numerous imaginative interpretations of God's involvement with creation.[33]

This has been my observation all along, that God-talk resorts to scriptural archetypes common to the collective unconscious of the believing community. This was made most manifest in our discussion of C. S. Lewis' struggles after the loss of his wife. The faith community, utilizing its collective imagery of God as found in hymns and scripture, tried to comfort Lewis with their God-talk. Lewis' struggle came in making the shift from logic to myth, from reason *(Logos)* to metaphor.

Metaphor, according to Green, is the key to interpreting God and thus the key in religious language. Green points out that religious language "is speech arising out of commitment to specific religious paradigms" embodied in a canon of scripture and "expressed in the life of a religious community." Because "*religion* is imaginative, religious language is metaphorical"; therefore, its "*theology* is hermeneutical." Literalists denied the imaginative character of the scriptures while liberals confused the issue by placing experience before imagination. This made experience the "criterion for revelation rather than the other way around." This is exactly what happens in the pastoral misinterpretation of God-talk. We take our theological agenda to God-talk and try to force the irregular edges of God-talk to fit in neat doctrinal theological shapes rather than listening to the experience that God-talk describes and then going to scripture for an interpretive paradigm. Thus, theology, according to Green, is hermeneutical, not metaphorical, which counters the claim made by Dorrien. Theology interprets the metaphorical language of religious life which, for Christians, is based on biblical paradigms. This is the method I have employed in my own interpretation of God-talk.[34]

Green then anticipates a question we have already confronted, that of fact versus fiction. Metaphor implies fiction for many of us in this fact-oriented society. Metaphor versus fact implies the dichotomy of fiction versus history. This is seen, according to Green, in the construction "is . . . is not." A religious event either is or is not historical. Some have moved beyond this dichotomy by suggesting that we use the construction "as if . . ." but Green notes perceptively that this is no better because the "move to 'as if' may soften the negative implications of 'is not,' suggesting that fictions have useful functions to fulfill, but the underlying dichotomy remains unchanged. . . ." Green suggests we instead use "as." Thus, we need to move into the realm of analogy, yet another literary category. "The point of using *as* is heuristic: not to affirm that something is or is not the case but rather to draw attention to one possibility among others by proposing an analogy."[35]

We move into Capps' categories of first and second order change as Green cites Ricouer's distinction between "first naïveté" and "second naïvéte." The person who exemplifies first naïveté lives in the world of, "is" and with this assured knowledge is unaware of any other possibilities. Those who exemplify second naïveté live in the realm of "as," and thus they are open to various meanings of interpretation because they are willing to imagine new possibilities. Green wisely notes that such an interpretive methodology risks relativism, but it seems that if one is guided by a scriptural paradigm that is itself filled with paradigms that conflict with each other, then this relativism will not be as dangerous as Green thinks.[36]

Green goes on to note that the key issue is whether the text's author is trustworthy or not. Can the sufferer, in the case of pastoral care, trust the religious imagination of the biblical author? Faith must therefore guide the person to choose to believe in the various paradigms present in the varied stories of the biblical text.[37] This emphasis on choice is a major task often unrecognized in pastoral care, especially in the realm of suffering. From a spiritual perspective, choice is often the key to understanding how and why people use God-talk. People faithfully choose to use God-talk, people faithfully choose to believe in God-talk, and people faithfully choose to believe in the biblical paradigms that help interpret God-talk. Thus, people trustingly, faithfully choose to move from first order to second order change in their grief period. As we have seen already, God-talk may be the very impetus that helps them make this important choice.

Green, addressing the task of pastoral care, notes that, in order to facilitate this process, the caregiver must be open to the imagination and the imagery of the biblical text. "The faithful imagination learns to hear the melody of revelation in the polyphony of scripture." We have already witnessed this methodology in the preceding chapter, and in the following pages, we will proceed in more detail as we investigate different biblical paradigms and their functions within the task of caregiving and the God-talk of the sufferer.[38]

From the previous discussion, it is clear that God-talk is theology voiced in and by the heart in a time of *angst*. This God-talk is manifest in myths produced by the religious imagination in order to relate what has happened to one caught in tragedy. Rather than employing the usual theological rhetoric of reason and logic, God-talk myths instead voice the experience in the more poetic terms of paradox, ambiguity, analogy, and emotion. As one uses God-talk to render into language what has happened, he looks to other imaginative experiences in the scripture of the faith community to find similar faith expressions. Imagination, analogy, paradox, ambiguity, and other literary categories help us to put together our experiences of tragedy (and good) into a myth that can then be interpreted by theologians (caregivers) into a greater picture of God. With this A-rational knowledge we can then move from our first naïveté, our first order change to second order change, which will facilitate healthy growth in the time of grief. God-talk begins this process and ends it as well with a new myth of God for the sufferer.

With this theoretical basis for God-talk in place, we will now move into a more imaginative interpretation of various depictions of God in order to demonstrate how God-talk is indeed based on solid biblical foundation.

Chapter 3

God-Talk and the Storms of Life

Inevitably we will encounter a comment from a sufferer equating tragedy with storms. In other contexts we might be called upon to interpret why natural disasters come upon unsuspecting people. Paradox abounds in such discussions as illustrated in the following example. God-talk expressed in the context of the storms of life presents the caregiver with a myriad of possibilities to interpret.

For example, what do we do with people who say they experience God's tremendous power and authority, not to mention care and security, during thunderstorms? People see the rainbow as a sign of God's promise to never flood the whole earth again, but what do we do with others who come to us and cry in disbelief over why God would send such flooding rains to their community and take away so many homes? Along with this, what do we do with those who say they witness the awesomeness of God in the calm after the storm when others are still picking up the pieces from the tornadoes or the hurricanes?

God-talk may take the metaphorical form of storm-talk in the pastoral conversation and caregivers need to be aware of the dynamics behind such language. People often talk of the storms of life when referring to marital problems, loss of jobs, a presidential crisis, or just life in general. Even phrases such as "every cloud has a silver lining" or "rainy days and Mondays" are presented to us during pastoral conversations.

Some people may even suggest that what our immoral country needs is a few storms to bring us back to a more divine focus. "What this country needs is a good recession" is often heard on the lips of those who, in other contexts would normally say, "I hope our children never have to go through something like that again." In my ministry, in rural areas I have heard farmers, during times of intense seasonal drought say, "What we need is a good hurricane" to break the drought. This was voiced quite often in 1999 when two years of drought had hurt the rural economy. Although farmers do not wish destruction to come upon their neighbors such as Hurricane Floyd brought to one-third of North Carolina, they know that the destructive forces of hurricanes also bring with them much needed, drought-busting rain. Thus, storm-talk is a quite confusing, paradoxical phenomenon to consider.

We must keep in mind that, biblically speaking, storms are part of God's responses to our lives. The prophets of ancient Israel periodically used storm talk in their divine threats against God's chosen nation. Isaiah 28 describes the coming attack of Assyria in stormy images. In Jeremiah 4, the attack of the Babylonians is compared to the hot desert siroccos that regularly devastate Palestine. The Book of Amos is rife with allusions to natural disasters. Some of Job's afflictions were connected to natural elements such as fire from the sky and strong winds, and God's tremendous epiphany to Job came in the context of a whirlwind. The psalmist used storm imagery to describe afflictions as the oppression of the enemy or wicked people (Psalms 55:8).

God is often portrayed in stormy images. God comes to Mount Sinai in ways that are quite suggestive of lightning storms or even volcanoes, according to the ways some scholars interpret Exodus 19. God guides the Israelites through the wilderness in a pillar of cloud by day and a pillar of fire by night. In 1 Kings 18, Elijah sees and experiences God in a way that can be best described as a horrendous meteorological storm. In the New Testament, Jesus and John of Patmos describe God's eventual coming through the images of storms and destruction.

There is clearly a connection between God and natural phenomenon throughout the Bible, and my contention here is that these images, and their psycho-religious archetypes are the background of the storm-talk that we encounter in God-talk. Understanding this religious phenomenon and being aware of the biblical foundations of such language informs the pastoral caregiver concerning the proper use of storm imagery, and this understanding will help us to interpret and even to use such God-talk in our pastoral conversations.

RESPONSES TO STORM-TALK

Unfortunately, however, when caregivers encounter such storm imagery, their responses may fall far short of being understanding. Such responses leave the client or parishioner with something less than adequate pastoral care. These responses are usually the result of the mistaken thinking that God does not send us storms,[1] but we have already seen in previous pages that we need to rethink this theology.

For example, if we consider the "Jesus Saves" illustration from the Introduction, we note that many times when this type of response is encountered in a pastoral context the caregiver might answer with, "Was God not with those who died in the storms?" This response is made to help people see how irresponsible their God-talk is regarding the whole situation. I would argue, however, that this kind of pastoral response may itself be quite irresponsible depending on the particular context. While this form of God-talk does sting in the face of others' personal losses, for *survivors* it is perhaps the only way to make sense of their survival when all else around them has been destroyed. Here we need to recall Macquarrie's focus on the total context of the theological encounter with sufferers and make our pastoral responses accordingly.

In the aftermath of a storm survival sufferers might acknowledge that God has saved them and then ask questions as to why they were saved. The conversation might then move to the implications of this survival, as if God has some purpose for their lives. This is a typical reaction to the tragedy and survival voiced by survivors, but responses to such questioning may leave survivors in the cold of despair. One pastoral response I heard in this situation was, "Perhaps you should wait until a later time to ponder this." While there is much wisdom in such a response, it may suggest to survivors that their immediate questions are out of place or even irrelevant.

In the case of positive storm-talk, a person may say, "I feel the power of God during thunderstorms." This was voiced to me by a highly educated man who liked to walk on his porch during thunderstorms in order to "be close to God's majesty." Some pastoral counselors may wonder why we must perceive God as so powerful. Might a loving God who is less threatening be a better image to adopt? Thus we may nod our heads in mock agreement to such God-talk, all the while belittling the person's theology and sense of the deity.

All of these pastoral responses betray a bias that God does not really inhabit storms. If we look at religion from a phenomenological perspective, we have to explain why people from primitive times to the present and from all walks of life tend to speak of the deity in storm images. Just because we disagree with this does not mean it is not a valid metaphor for God. It may, in fact, reveal that we have not made peace with this very disturbing aspect of deity.

These responses also neglect three aspects of God's interactions with humans. First, they deny God's control over the earth. As we will see in a later chapter on apocalyptic imagery, there is a very important pastoral reason why God is depicted in storm images. If God is not in control of an earth that seems out of control, then the sufferer is ultimately left with more chaos to answer to, not less. This alternative is not very consoling. From another perspective, we cannot prove God does not come to earth to act upon people through storms. Thus, it is misleading for us to say that God does not act in such deeds.

Second, such pastoral responses ignore the numerous biblical passages where God does indeed send torments, punishments, and storms upon people for specific purposes.[2] The stories of Joseph and Job immediately come to mind here. These stories clearly state that God was behind the scenes manipulating the situation in order to bring about a Divine Good. From the New Testament perspective, we can think of both Jesus and Paul where dire circumstances led to the furthering of the Kingdom. It can be argued that these biblical texts are looking back with the advantage of hindsight, and thus are able to interpret the good that the incident brought about. It could also be argued that, if such hindsight was not acceptable in religious circles, it would not have been allowed to become scripture. Along with this, some caregivers think such storm passages and storm-talk reflect "primitive" religion, but this begs the question: Primitive as compared to what? Does this suggest that faith communities that have the benefits of scriptures are reflective and that oral communities are thus somewhat ignorant or unreflective? Such pejorative thinking does not belong in the pastoral encounter.

Third, and most important, these responses neglect the theological reason behind such comments. In the eyes of our parishioners and clients, they have endured or survived a tempest while others did not. Or, they realized that the storms they lived through brought about spiritual growth and insight. They may question the storms in light of their past goodness, or they may honestly feel that these storms were sent to lead them back from straying paths. Whether it be survival or spiritual growth, the question of a reason for this particular storm eventually arises. Those who choose to see God's hand in all of life's circumstances, good or bad, see the hand of God in both storms and rainbows. Sufferers who try to put their experiences into perspective deserve caregivers who understand not only God-talk that comes in the metaphors of storm images, but also a God who comes to us through the storms of life.

SPIRITUAL DYNAMICS OF SURVIVORS

D. W. Foy notes in the *Dictionary of Pastoral Care and Counseling* the potential problems that are related to survivors of disasters.[3] In such instances there are three stages of grief: Impact, Recoil, and Reorganization. In the Impact stage, disorientation, denial, disbelief, and helplessness are often visible signs of spiritual chaos in the life of a survivor. "This can't be happening to me, I am so confused about things, nothing makes sense to me, I feel so utterly alone" are typical responses we hear from sufferers of natural tragedies or experiences that seem stormy in the greater picture of life.

Once the storm has passed, signs of grief, anger, hostility, depression as well as abandonment and helplessness along with the need for blame are seen in the recoil stage. During this time, the sufferers will begin to see the disparity in their theology and the reality that is now upon them. The need to modify their perceptions of life circumstances so that these may be viewed without sufferers moving into the sphere of victimization will loom on the horizon of recovery. Part of this reorganization process involves the honest assessment of shattered life assumptions. David K. Switzer, standing on the conclusions of Anton Boisen, notes that this time of reinterpretation moves sufferers into a higher cognitive level of faith development. "The higher level meant a reintegration of the individual's personality, bringing greater insight, new perspectives, and additional strength." This reorientation would lead the individual to focus on his or her life around a new center.[4] It should be quite apparent that this time of reorganization leads to new perspectives on God, and thus a new faith and belief system as well. As we will see, this is what happened to Job.

The God-talk encountered in the time of tragedy and the following days of recovery can help lead the sufferer through this time of confusion. God-talk is admittedly paradoxical and this ambiguity can demonstrate to the sufferer the inadequacy (or the accuracy!) of previous theologies to interpret the present problem. Part of this cognitive reappraisal includes comparison of one's situation to that of other survivors and victims. Searching for spiritual meaning, whether through the scriptures, discussions, or therapy is often part of the process, and this search involves the judicious use, understanding of, and acceptance of God-talk that incorporates storm imagery. As victims reorganize their poststorm lives, they also reorganize their theological assumptions. A God who was originally seen as good and loving may now be seen realistically as the agent of the disaster. If so, what does this say about God? Did the sufferer not previously consider such an aspect of God's character and temperament?

Such times of questioning one's previous theological assumptions indicate a need for, and perhaps require, a reexamination of one's God images. Perhaps this picture has been rather immature, consisting of spiritual stick figures from childhood Bible lessons. Looking for clues as to why God has done such a terrible thing leads to introspection and talking with others who have survived disaster. This is an important ritual, the walking through the valley of the shadow discussed earlier, that survivors must work through as they try to make sense of their personal predicament. Caregivers can help by relating biblical examples of God's involvement in storm-related appearances.

BIBLICAL EXAMPLES OF GOD-INDUCED STORMS

We can look to the Bible for a paradigm that will help us explain stormy events to our troubled parishioners. Such an investigation reveals the religious and ritualistic needs of such imagery.

As we begin this examination, we must first realize that the God of the Old Testament, known as Yahweh, was once believed to be a storm God. Mark S. Smith's examination of this topic is illuminating for this discussion.[5] The Israelites described Yahweh using the attributes of the Phoenician deity Baal and it is most probable that there was some confusion concerning these deities because they were so similar. Since Baal was depicted in storm images, the Israelites soon assimilated these attributes into their own descriptions of their deity Yahweh. Interestingly, Smith notes that this took place as part of a political move by the dominant ruling powers of that day. It was designed to persuade followers of Baal to follow Yahweh, the only true God. Smith notes that, throughout the history of God in Israel, each change of the political administration brought with it a change in the attributes of the deity. During these potentially stormy times in Israel's history, days that witnessed much social unrest and thus induced anxiety in the everyday life of the people of Israel, changes in the theological depiction of the deity were part of the process.

If we think through the various pastoral problems of such a time we can see some parallels to modern day pastoral situations with which we are presented. Stormy times in the life of an individual, a community, a state, or a country bring with them renewed interpretations of the deity. Sometimes it is the initial presentations of a new image of the deity that spark such unrest; at other times, however, it is the unrest that triggers the renewed investigations of the God images in a society. In the context of pastoral care it is academic to argue which brings about the other. The point for caregivers here is that dramatic changes in life, be they political, social, personal, or even religious, force us to confront old God images in light of the new reality of life.[6]

We witnessed this during the Gulf War Desert Storm campaign. Evangelicals were quick to point out that God was behind the successful military campaign. God was the mighty warrior, quick to defend the powerless. Liberal theologians, however, were reluctant to adopt such an image of God. Instead, they portrayed God as loving and compassionate, One who hurt for the lost lives of the Iraqi people as well. Both sides quoted scripture to justify their positions and the whole debate occurred during a time of political confusion and potential global instability.

The conservatives were responding to the prevalent liberal opinion of our legislators; thus, they argued in favor of war. The liberal response was that war was not necessary. Interestingly, when the crisis in Kosovo arose, the two sides switched in their theology. Conservatives were staunchly against the war while liberals claimed God's justice was necessary to stop the Serbian ethnic cleansing of the Albanians. Crisis and instability bring out conflicting versions of God and ambiguous versions of God-talk. Context determines which version is "correct."

Smith goes on to note that Baal and Yahweh were described as storm gods and mighty warriors. Both designations went hand in hand. As warriors, Baal or Yahweh would take on the powers of the underworld or hold in check the mighty waters of death. Such battles were, paradoxically, mythical wars reenacted on earth on the battle lines of enemies and in the religious confrontations between nations. The god of the victor was seen as the ruler of both heaven and earth.

Thus, we see that God is no stranger to storm imagery. It should therefore come as no surprise that God would make use of storms to bring messages to the people on earth and that people would incorporate such imagery into their God-talk. In the story of Jonah, we see clearly how a storm is interpreted to be a messenger from God. Jonah is called, indeed commanded to "Get up and go to Ninevah." Instead, he runs in the opposite direction to the coast. The image is a mirror of everyday life. We have only to listen to testimonials from believers to see the parallels.

"I felt like God wanted me to do X but I ran the other way. Then this (tragedy, storm, crash, etc.) happened, and it made me realize that I was running away from God." We often hear such words from people we encounter. Whether we agree with the person's conclusions or not, it is clear that, in the person's opinion, the tragic event brought about the change that led to the pursuit of God's desired plan for his or her life. The tragedy presented the person with a choice: either do God's will or accept the consequences. The person's religious experience here cannot be questioned. It happened, and we must interpret it as valid. How do we understand the implications and help the person to comprehend them as well?

It is obvious in the account of Jonah that God is using the storm to tell Jonah something. In Chapter 1:4 we read, "So Yahweh hurled a great wind upon the seas . . ." (my translation) and it was this great wind (*ruach:* spirit, wind) that produced the sea storm. The image of God's *ruach* is familiar to most biblical interpreters. Recall the spirit of God moving across the face of the Deep, chaotic waters that would soon be commanded into the orderly Creation in Genesis 1. This image of the wind of God blowing over the chaotic waters is fully examined by Jon D. Levenson.[7] He relates that these are the same waters that periodically get loose from their underworld prison (Job 38:8-11, for example) and create havoc (interpreted "tragedy") on the earthlings. The psalmist uses similar imagery throughout the psalms when depicting the enemies surrounding him or the dark days of despair and crisis that occasionally haunt him.

This image of God and wind and storms is not new, and it is one that should indeed be quite familiar to us and our clients and parishioners. It should come as no surprise when people relate to us that God has sent them a storm or that trials were given to them by God. This is what is related in the story of Jonah.

Jack Sasson, in his commentary on Jonah, provides several thoughts concerning the use of storm imagery in ancient literature.[8] He notes that "storms permitted the writer to ponder the cosmic significance behind such cataclysms by singly or successively contrasting the benevolence accorded the survivor to the punishment meted out. . . ." As we have seen in our discussion of the grief process of storm survivors, this is exactly what pastoral theologians tell us happens when people, in the aftermath of storms and disasters, begin to ponder anew their old god-images in light of their new circumstances. It seems ancient religious writers were employing storm imagery to force their readers to do what victims of storms and disasters must do in the aftermath of their personal tragedies. This is an important paradigm for caregivers to consider in their approaches to sufferers as well.

Sasson goes on to note that in ancient literature, survivors of storms were thought to have been "graced by the gods" either for personal gain or for religious purposes. I have observed this same phenomenon where those who survived terrible tragedies are often thought to be special, blessed, or even higher than life in the eyes of "regular people." Anyone who survives a fiery plane crash, a series of destructive tornados, or devastating floods, not to mention cancer or a car crash, must certainly be blessed. I also have noticed in my ministry that these survivors are sought out by people who have just survived similar tragedies, as if they might provide some wisdom to help interpret what has happened. It is as if ordinary people, those who have not suffered similar tragedy, cannot understand what the sufferer/survivor is searching for. Only those who have faced death and come out on the other side of tragedy can truly communicate with those who have been through similar circumstances.

At the same time, Sasson relates that those in the ancient world who did not survive the tragedy are seen as deserving of their fate. This is not just an ancient phenomenon. Witness how people today will make comments such as, "I just knew Joe's drinking would be his downfall" or "If she would have just given her life to the Lord instead of running off after those foolish dreams of hers" or "We told them not to build by the river." I would also add that in ancient times, victims of tragedies were often seen as unwitting instruments in the greater will of the gods. In other words, they were sacrifices. This feeling can be seen today when we hear somebody say, "Those people shouldn't have died that way, but now maybe some good will come of it." This notion of sacrifice is one way to find an answer to questions that are beyond answers altogether.

STORMS AS AGENTS OF GOD'S PLAN

There are other biblical examples of storms as part of God's overall plan for humankind. In the flood, all humankind is seen to be corrupt, despite their previous good and very good status. The same God who created the earth and its inhabitants is now ready to destroy the creation with a mighty deluge. The Hebrew text of Genesis 6:13, while problematic and confusing, is quite poignant: So God said to Noah, "An end to all flesh on it [the earth] comes before me. Because the earth is filled with violent wrongdoing from them [earthlings], behold I will corrupt them by way of the earth" (my translation).

It is clear that the earth is the agent of God's destruction of the creation. This is accomplished as the rainwaters from on high are unleashed through heaven's windows and the terrible waters of the Deep are released from below the earth (Genesis 7:11). They converge in one devastating storm that destroys all creation save Noah, his family, and the animals on the ark. All creation was sacrificed despite its theologically good status and a new beginning was made. We can only imagine Noah's feelings after the flood. Overwhelming emotions of gratitude no doubt clashed with huge tides of guilt for being the only ones good enough to be saved from the destruction. This text would be an excellent passage to use for meditation and instruction for those who have suffered similar losses and experienced the same emotions.

We have dealt with apocalyptic images in our discussion of God-talk in another chapter but it will serve our purpose well to be reminded here of the use of stormy scenarios in the apocalyptic vocabulary. Many commentators have struggled with the image of God portrayed in Revelation.[9] Here God destroys major portions of the earth in order to bring about retribution for the evil rampant on the earth. Those under persecution from the whims of life can easily associate with this theology. They understand the constant trials of just trying to be good people in this seemingly evil world. Many will faithfully state that their problems are just part of the larger plan of God and that they must endure the trials of this world until the world to come removes them from such persecution. Thus, they may refer to the last days when God comes in glory and proves that divine actions were part of the overall plan of life.

In the New Testament, we encounter several storm experiences. Paul's shipwreck is mentioned twice, once in Acts 27 and also in 2 Corinthians 11:25-26. The story in Acts is highly embellished and shares many similarities with other Hellenistic accounts of tragedy at sea. The brief mention in 2 Corinthians offers no immediate commentary, yet each of these accounts has been compared by scholars to the story of Jonah. When reflecting on the shipwreck tragedy of Paul, we also must bear in mind the lessons learned from the discussion of Jonah. At the same time, it is clear from reading both Acts and Paul's letters that the authors firmly believe God's hand was at work in this tragedy. Indeed, the tragedy worked to further the Kingdom of God. It appears from this that it is not the tragedy so much as the choice of interpretation given to the tragedy after the fact that determines the positive or negative spiritual growth of the sufferer. Certainly Paul provides us with a positive example of how to see God's will in the storms of life.

As sufferers work through the terrible psychological trauma that surrounds a tragic event, it might be efficacious to lead them through other tragic figures from the scriptures as they explore their feelings and reactions to their own tragedy. In the story of Joseph in Genesis, the reader is told throughout the tale, both from the narrator's point of view and through the character of Joseph himself, that it was God's will that he suffer *so that* the Hebrew people would survive the famine in the land of Palestine. Initially this line of thought may not be uplifting for the sufferer, but if this passage is coupled with 1 Peter, then the sufferer may see that suffering has many positive merits once the sufferer begins to look beyond his or her own personal circumstance. In 1 Peter the author reminds readers that suffering has positive merits. Christ suffered, so the sufferer is in good company with others who have suffered worse fates. Thus, the sufferer should rejoice! Incidentally, when pastoral caregivers use the consoling words, "Just remember there are others who have it worse than you" or when sufferers say, "Whenever I think about my situation I think that others have it worse than me," they are recalling the same line of reasoning that Peter uses in his pastoral letter to fellow sufferers (1 Peter).

Paul wrestled with such ideas of unjust retribution by God and some of his disturbing conclusions may be found in Romans 9 in which he writes that God endures vessels of wrath made for the good of others. Apparently borrowing imagery from Job, Paul asks who we think we are that we should question God's motives. Does the pot refute the potter's intentions? Are not functional pots also made from the same clay as decorative ones? In this line of reasoning, we begin to see a pervading thread of grace running throughout this passage. In God's incomprehensible plan, the ultimate rule of grace often requires the temporal use of punishment and even injustice according to our standards. Despite our feelings on the subject, God acts according to God's plan. It is we who must learn to accept this plan for our lives. And the school of suffering is often the only place of instruction for these very difficult lessons of life.

The Psalms provide many illustrations for the sufferer to walk through.[10] In Psalm 18, we sing the hymn of one who suffered a tremendous storm in life. Interestingly, in this psalm, we sing that God *saved* the psalmist by sending a storm. Here the singer is caught in the ropes of death, indeed, in torrents of waters. These torrents reflect the real life situation of many in Palestine who know that heavy rains in the hills result in lightning quick flash floods that descend through the dry wadi. There is no warning of such floods and those caught in them would surely perish. God hears the cry of the drowning victim who is sinking ever deeper into the underwater world of the terrible chaotic Deep. Instead of gently lifting up the lost singer, however, God creates a counter storm to produce the salvation of the storm-tossed soul (vv. 7-15). Hail and thunder coupled with smoke, quakes, and lightning literally blow away the raging waters of death and dry out the muddy riverbed.

Here is a clear instance where God, according to the psalmist's posttrauma spiritual assessment of the event, sent a storm to deliver one from a storm. Victims of tragedy may find this poem insightful as they wade through the confusing issues surrounding multiple tragedies. In Psalm 42, however, we sing that God's powerful waves have overflowed the psalmist, causing much despair. "Why has God forsaken me?" the psalmist laments. In a confusing way, verse 8 of this psalm interrupts the negative sense of the psalm by suddenly offering up praise to the very deity the psalmist accuses of creating the present tragedy. The text of Psalm 42 is so negative that the positive spin of verse 8 seems to be an addition to the psalm.[11] Why are interpreters, both biblical and pastoral, so quick to question praise in the context of pain?

We should note that many of our sufferers who speak of how God has sent them terrible storms will turn right around and speak of God in exalting terms. Praise amid despair often catches caregivers off guard, but in the realm of God-talk, it makes perfectly good sense for two reasons. First, focusing on the positives, even though they be few, helps to generate positive energy to the soul, and this small "pick-me-up" may be the one or even the only thing that carries the sufferer through the tragedy. Second, if we examine this situation in the greater realm of religion, especially mythology, we see a reason why people may be reluctant to cry out to God. If you think God is behind the destruction you are facing, which course would you take, offering a nugget of praise in the hope that God might lessen the storm or hurling critical abuse at God in the hope that stinging accusations might turn the situation around?

In Psalm 68, we sing of an instance where God's comforting presence is witnessed and even felt in storms. Here the psalmist recounts the wilderness experience. It is a terrible time for the struggling new nation as Moses and the Israelites experience the many wiles of the wilderness for the first time. There is no water or food, and signs of God's presence, despite the mighty miracle at the Red Sea, are few and far between. Yet the psalmist reminds the congregation that God was there in the tremblings of the earth, the rains that fell, and even the quaking of Mount Sinai. These potentially frightening natural occurrences are, in the context of worship and the praise of salvation, given a new interpretation: that of being part of God's creative will.

The Book of Job provides one of the most striking cases for the appearance of God as a storm during times of personal struggle. While many who come to us believe that God is calm, rational, and let us say, theologically neat, Job saw a side of God that was exactly the opposite. He meets a God who is irrational, blustery, and theologically dirty. Job is described as a righteous man, one so righteous, in fact, that he even makes sacrifices for his family, lest they slip and fail to appease God. In what amounts to a bet between God and the Satan, a figure whose task it is to make accusations against the earthlings in a test of their faith in God, Job becomes the unwitting pawn in a game played between these two cosmic figures.

The conditions of the bet are simple. The Satan, that is, the Accuser, may inflict any harm on Job that he desires, as long as he does not take Job's life. Job's possessions, wealth, and family are then destroyed by marauders or by natural stormy events. Then the Satan attacks Job himself, inflicting him with medical problems and reducing him to a whiny, bent over, and defeated shell of a believer.

We can stop right here and note that many come to us and complain that they feel they are nothing but game pieces on the board of life, moved about indiscriminately by forces they cannot see. Thus, the Book of Job is an excellent scripture to employ in discussing how life seems irrational and how we feel out of control of our lives. Compared to this scripture, then, the sufferers' inclinations, as manifest in their God-talk, are exactly right! Thus, many sufferers are filled with the same confusion and questions that Job experienced during his tragedy and time of testing.

Job, however, fights back (despite Psalm 42!), accusing God of breaking from the religious traditions that were prevalent in this time. The religious thinking was simple: do good and you would be blessed, do bad and God would curse.[12] The wealth and the notoriety of Job reveal that he had done good deeds and that God had blessed him very much. Thus, the theological tension in the story leads us to ask: Why has all of this destruction fallen upon him? What has gone wrong?

Job makes his case, correctly accusing God of breaking the rules. Why has evil fallen upon one who has done only good all of his life? Job's well-intended friends counter his accusations against the deity as well as his own self-righteousness. They suggest (incorrectly, the reader soon learns) that God would never allow such evil to fall upon someone unless he deserved it. In essence, they are saying that Job must have done something wrong because God always acts according to the rules. In other words, God is always rational. Thus, Job had best reconsider his claim that he is righteous and God is wrong.

This argument is made throughout the book until Chapter 38 when God has finally had enough questioning by Job. Job has demanded an audience, indeed, a trial of God. So God gives in and appears, but not in the usual way we think God would appear. "Then the LORD answered Job out of the storm . . ." we read in Job 38:1, and for the next several chapters God dismantles Job's and, consequently, our rational beliefs and assumptions about God. In essence, God tells Job, "I am God; you are human. Get over it. You don't tell me how to run this creation; I tell creation how to run your life. Life does not go the way you think it should go. It moves the way I tell it to, whether you understand it or not."

These are not comforting words at all, either for Job or for us. Those who feel God should not test them or hurt them display the sin of presumptuousness, that is, the presumption that they are above such indignities. The book of Job reveals that all may be victims of God's whims, both the good and the bad, the righteous one and the sinner. In our self-absorbed society, this revelation may come as a shock, but it may also be the first step toward a major life change on the part of the sufferer. Tragedy brings about much humiliation, and this may very well be the divine purpose of such events in life. Humility reminds us of our need for God.

Some good comes from this stormy confrontation. God tells Job that his accusations against the deity are true! This admission does not change God's revelation of how creation runs, but it does provide some solace to the suffering Job and to those who suffer today, if we care to amend our theologies to fit reality. If God admits to irrational acts, then we must alter our rational theologies to fit God's plan. As many sufferers and survivors of tragedy often, if perhaps reluctantly, admit, they have a whole new understanding of life based on what they have experienced. They, like Job, have seen a different side of God and, as with any life-threatening or life-changing encounter with God, their lives, along with their theology, change with such encounters.[13]

The point of this chapter is this: in the middle of this personal tale of tragedy and amid the consequent questions of doubt and anger, God answers Job not in the tidy, loquacious, and erudite pedantics of theological rhetoric, but instead dirties Job's theological need for neatness with a whirlwind that is a storm. Likewise, God speaks to us in storm-talk and many respond with a similar vocabulary. Thus, it is important for caregivers to understand the dynamics and nuances of storm-talk.

It is the whirlwind that sufferers and caregivers often try to avoid in the aftermath of trials. We want to understand God through our rational, reasoned, and theologically astute definitions, but in the reality of storms, we find that these explanations of God are nothing but idolatries built with the gold, silver, and wood of Enlightenment thought.[14] We see here in the story of Job that it is the very irrational, tumultuous, and terrifying whirlwind that reveals the true nature of God and, eventually, calms the distraught Job. We should note that it is his acceptance of this revelation of God's true self that quiets his pleas and confusions and that only with this compliance, with this new understanding of God, the initial losses Job suffered are then restored. The restoration of these losses implies that with Job's understanding of God, Job's life will return to normal and he will find God's true blessing through this new understanding.

It is in the whirlwind, the storm, that our questions as to who or what God really is are finally answered. Similarly, it is through the storms of life that our souls can eventually find the peace that passes all understanding. Understanding that God throws storms at us and that God has reasons for doing so is part of the greater mysteries of life that we must learn to accept. Those who do so make peace with this aspect of God, as their God-talk often reveals.

Once the sufferer realizes that the biblical picture of God is indeed centered around storms, then a new understanding of God can be initiated and incorporated into the life of the victim. The powerful story of Jesus calming the storm at night on the Sea of Galilee (Mark 4:36-41; Matt 8:23-27; Luke 8:22-25) provides a paradigm of hope for the struggling sufferer. Here Jesus, God-in-the-flesh, is in the boat with the disciples. A storm quickly rages down upon the hapless followers. We should not miss the mythical aspects of this story. It is night, a time when demons come out. Night also symbolizes the chaotic darkness reminiscent of the precreation in Genesis 1. The waters are the dangerous chaotic waters that seek to break their bonds (Job 38:8-11) and wreak havoc upon the earth.

Jesus is asleep in the boat, a sign that storms which frighten and threaten earthlings do not bother God at all. Indeed, it appears that God is asleep on the job! But keep in mind what we have discussed in this chapter. God is the creator of storms, according to the Old Testament, and God apparently has no qualms about sending them out upon the unsuspecting creation. The disciples, however, are in a frenzy, and well they should be. Their very lives are at stake!

They awaken Jesus and, realizing that the storm is frightening his friends, he tells the storm "Quiet! Be still!" (Mark 4:39 NIV). The disciples, upon witnessing this amazing display of power, ask in terrified fear, "Who is this?" The answer, for the reader and the sufferer is plain. *This* is God, and in the Jewish mind-set of the early followers of Jesus, it was understood that this God could send storms at any time. But, as they had just witnessed, this God may also calm storms when necessary.

God allows storms to blow our way in order to further the creative purpose, as the Israelites, the psalmists, or the readers of Revelation believed. The psalmist sings, "Our God is in the heavens; he does whatever he pleases" (Psalm 115:3 RSV), and Paul faithfully writes "What shall we say then? Is there injustice on God's part? By no means!" (Romans 9:14 RSV). When sufferers come to us relating, complaining, or just remarking about the storms in life and how God has used these storms to bring about change in their lives, we should rejoice. Like Elijah, they have stood on the edge of life itself and witnessed the awesome power of this stormy God pass by in lightning, quakes, and wind. They have learned, by listening to the still small voice that comes in the calm after the storm, one of the most difficult lessons in life, because they have confronted the most mysterious being in the Creation.

Chapter 4

God-Talk As Myth

Thus far we have examined various forms of God-talk phrases within their pastoral contexts. We have noted that this phenomenon has a language, perhaps even a vocabulary, of its own and that it must be understood within its own particular personal context. We have also seen that using the category of myth helps us to understand God-talk and that theology has steered away from this category rather than embrace it as viable religious language. Imagination, as witnessed in various literary genres, is key to understanding myth, and, thus, God-talk in its various genres as well. With this in mind, it is now time to explore the irrational language of myth that, I believe, is the very basis for God-talk.

GOD-TALK, MYTH, AND THE CONFRONTATION WITH EVIL

We have noted that God-talk in the pastoral conversation often arises when the speaker is confronted with what most of our society, including theologians, calls "evil." Storms, death, sickness, famine, disease, tragedy, and other catastrophes are often uncritically lumped together into the category of "evil." Sufferers, when buffeted by these ill winds, come to us for guidance and comfort or just to make sense of the confusing situation. Morton Kelsey provides a model that is helpful in this examination of God-talk. From his experience with people who confront evil in a spiritual manner, he suggests that our rational, scientific methods of interpretation are not adequate to understand what can only be called the irrational experiences of humans. Thus, he looks to the broad category of myth for the proper tools to understand the experience of evil.[1]

At the outset, we must admit that his and our definition of evil are not an exact match. He suggests that there are four descending categories of good and evil that humans experience. His categories will be briefly enumerated here. There is good, then there is good that can initially appear evil to those who struggle to see or accept it. Next, there is evil that can eventually appear good or even work toward good. Finally, there is evil itself. This is the category that Kelsey examines. This kind of evil is seen in the realm of the demonic, Black Magic and the worship of Satan, or in those who manifest the most psychotic of mental illnesses. Kelsey develops his interpretative model for this particular psychological phenomenon.[2]

For this study of God-talk, however, I have deliberately chosen not to investigate evil of this kind. It would appear that Kelsey's model might not be appropriate for our general pastoral ministry. However, we must keep in mind that, in the eyes of our parishioners, their particular experience of grief and tragedy may seem to them very evil. Their initial *perception* is that evil has befallen them. Along with this, seminary trained ministers and pastoral caregivers generally have studied the *problem of evil* and pastoral care books that explore the realm of suffering also term experiences of tragedy and crisis as evil Thus, pastoral caregivers generally will be approaching the pastoral dilemmas of their parishioners and clients from the initial perspective of "evil." With this in mind, Kelsey's model and observations will be a starting place for our present discussion.

Although evidence has been presented throughout this study that what we perceive as evil is simply part of God's plan for creation, part of our task in understanding God-talk is to help people realize that their very use of God-talk suggests that God, not the Devil or Fate or Chance, is ultimately behind their present circumstance. At the very least, God could be doing a better job in controlling the evil that is manifest in the present crisis. This also helps people distinguish between difficulties and problems, as delineated in our discussion of Capps' first and second order change. Sufferers must realize that the language they use to explain what has happened to them or what they perceive to have happened to them is not a rational language at all but an A-rational language that must be understood within that context.[3]

Kelsey, like Macquarrie, suggests that there are two ways people relate their experiences to us: through story and through reasoned thought. He perceptively notes that reasoned thought has no acceptable means for relating emotions, and caregivers, realizing that the pastoral context is filled with emotions, should take note of Kelsey's observation. This in itself should help us to understand once more that rational theologies and philosophies, such as the "problem of evil," simply cannot be applied with any effectiveness to the highly charged experiences of grief and tragedy. Along with this, Kelsey notes that people think in two different ways as well: through either unconscious or rational thoughts. From this we can see that, in the realm of the pastoral encounter, the caregiver will be presented with two possibilities: rational thought and its reasoned dispassionate approach to a very emotional issue and story with its myriad images that spew forth from the unconscious in an often confusing, nonrational, and emotional stream.

Based on experience, most pastoral encounters are centered around the issue of "evil" and how it has affected our parishioners or clients. The experience of this evil, Kelsey argues, is a spiritual experience, and, by the very laws of reasoned thought, spiritual experiences simply cannot be examined using the tools of modern, objective research, much less explained by them. Such attempts, although well-intended, prove futile in the end and, as we have seen, leave the sufferer feeling anything but assured or comforted. Rudolf Otto's *The Idea of the Holy* will help us to better understand what Kelsey suggests.

Writing against the objective trend in academic theological circles and countering the pietistic spirituality of the 1800s, Otto noted in 1924 that theologians generally describe only a rational God without giving proper attention to the *irrational* side of the deity. God is *numinous,* Otto suggests, that is, God resides outside of us, and therefore we are creatures and God is the Creator. Once this numinous quality of God is understood, it should lead to feelings of awe, tremors, and fears in the face of this *mysterium tremendum,* as Otto describes God. God has a merciful side, but God is also capable of tremendous wrath, as many biblical stories attest only too well. These traits, often seemingly capricious, lead to a sense of "awe-full majesty" which overwhelms the believer. The *creature* feels a sense of *creaturehood* which, in the face of the overwhelming power of God, makes the creature feel impotent and worthless. All of these attributes of God are combined by Otto into the adjective *holy* which does not mean only "goodness," as many today would interpret God, but also entails "awe-fullness." Thus, the complex category of "holy" itself is filled with both rational and irrational implications.[4]

Today's culture would disagree with Otto for many reasons. First, as has been noted throughout this discussion, we have been influenced by the scientific/rational mind-set which disparages mythical, fanciful, and irrational concepts of God. Second, while many today are turning to the spiritual realm in protest of this emphasis of rational interpretations of God, this phenomenon also has been misleading because the spiritual trend focuses only on finding God internally mimicking the superficiality of the self-help, pop-psychology movement. These two trends have led to a "dumbing down" of the idea of God's holiness which brings us to the third reason Otto's argument is not understood today. If God is rational and therefore good, as our Enlightenment-influenced world tends to believe, then this good God cannot bring about evil, which we have termed irrational in our rational world. In effect, our scientific, cultural, and spiritual society has limited God only to good things in our world and relegated evil to the realm of the devil, or worse, the nihilistic categories of Fate or Mother Nature or Life. Thus, in our theological worldview, God is incapable of wrath, evil, or even vengeance. We have, in effect, idolized God into an image of ourselves.

Tragically, the church is not immune to this process, and its theological leaders may be unwittingly fostering this dangerous trend. Ministers who are a byproduct of our culture are also no strangers to this way of thinking.[5] Theologian Carl E. Braaten, commenting on the various attempts to name God in the academic world, makes an observation on this phenomenon that is appropriate to our discussion as well. He warns that "we may succumb to the illusion that our artificial ways of speaking *about* God should dictate all other ways of speaking *for* God and *to* God."[6]

Given Otto's discussion of the irrational side of God and the current theological and pastoral critique of our society's misguided attempts to be spiritual and find God only within ourselves, it is quite important that we be careful in our naming of God and our limiting of the divine attributes of God. We may be creating more trouble than we think we are eliminating. The evidence presented thus far in this study of God-talk suggests that the depiction of God in God-talk, while apparently irrational and difficult to comprehend, not to mention stomach, is more realistic than our nice theological categories that package God neatly in the current socially, culturally, or politically correct box.

None of the experiences of tragedy—the sudden death of a loved one, the frightening diagnosis of cancer— can be restricted just to the realm of the rational. The God-talk that arises from these situations is an attempt to explain what has happened to the person. This attempt at an explanation is really the *perception* of the person. The perception may in fact be far from reasoned reality, and in this case, the caregiver helps the sufferer to work slowly back to the present reality. On the other hand, the perception is all we have to work with during the pastoral moment and that is the *reality* with which we must initially work. In this reality, the language is anything but rational because it is relating a nonrational and most likely emotional perception of a spiritual dilemma.

With this in mind we must resort to the nonrational. Here we leave axioms and proofs and encounter the more whimsical realm of story which, as we have already learned and Kelsey reminds us, is filled with images and symbols that are anything but rational. The caregiver must also enter the realm of myth, story, and symbol that arises from the unconscious if he or she is to really understand what the sufferer is talking about.

Kelsey makes several observations about myth that echo aspects we have already suggested or will touch on in the following pages. For example, he states that symbolic thinking comes from a "center of purpose within us." I take this to mean that there is a sense of the divine within us that we are not in touch with until the times of tragedy when the soul (the unconscious; the heart) reaches out and says what the mind (the conscious) cannot verbalize. Thus, God-talk is the language of the heart. This observation was verified when I noticed that the God-talk we are investigating arose only during times of crisis. It would appear that the heart, the soul, knows when to switch to a language more appropriate to the present experience. Kelsey goes on to suggest that this realm of thinking represents wisdom. I suggested earlier that God-talk that has been passed on to sufferers by those who have endured similar tragedies or has been offered as comforting words by older people who have witnessed many such experiences expresses a folk-type wisdom cherished in the community of faith. We will see below that the term "wisdom" appears again in other definitions of myth and this suggests that myth is part of a larger phenomenon of accumulated, experiential knowledge.[7]

With this in mind it is helpful to pause here and explore exactly what is meant by wisdom. While many attribute wisdom to the advancing of years, there is a growing consensus that real wisdom is the combining of *mythos* and *Logos,* that is, reason and story. Past thinkers have stressed reason, *Logos,* over myth, which is often deemed immature thought. Before logical processes dominated our minds, however, people believed their lives were directed by external, divine forces. Since the time of Plato, however, *Logos* has been the preferred mode of thought in the Western world. With this logical process the soul was seen as separate from the body. We could step back and observe in an objective way how life was happening to us. Myth, the actions of the gods, was demoted to fanciful, childish thought. This one-sided mode of thinking has dominated Western society, but current investigation into the world of wisdom now suggests that the mature person consists of a balance of both *Logos* and *mythos* that is seen in paradoxical tension within the person. In essence, experience and logic are in synthesis in the wise person.[8]

Wisdom believes in a simple way that a good God is the cause of all things.[9] This notion has been found in our discussion of the background of God-talk and its implications concerning the deity. I suggested earlier that God-talk may be a form of folk-wisdom that carries on wisdom from the ancient past. Evidence supports this assertion in that wisdom can be found in *memes* that are selected and transmitted across generations for at least eighty generations. Thus, in an archetypal sense, wisdom is located in our minds, our psyches, our souls. While science is a relatively late phenomenon, wisdom as encountered in religion, myth, and philosophy is ancient. Science is but one way to look at and make conclusions about life's experiences. Sometimes the clearer, scientific view is only a more narrow picture of the real situation. According to one study of wisdom, "The great 'width' (empathy), 'height' (intelligence), and 'depth' (reflectivity) of the wise person allows him or her to form a more complex or *concrete and abstract* perspective on some problem and thus attain the possibility of seeing the wisest course of action." We have certainly seen that, when explored fully, God-talk exemplifies this conclusion and rids us of the dilemma of making difficulties into problems. Thus, it would appear that the wise investigation of life's experiences allows for the best spiritual, psychological growth for an individual.[10]

Those who employ wise approaches to crisis situations are better able to tackle paradoxical problems. They are better able to face issues involving uncertainty and even contradictions. Yet wise people are also aware of the limits of their understanding and the ability to solve ill-defined problems. In other words, they are quite comfortable with mystery as an answer to their searches. Those who rely on logical approaches to such problems cannot acknowledge uncertainty. They try to explain it, turning difficulties into problems. Logic insists upon answers while myth and wisdom look at the problem and are willing to conclude that there is no answer at all.[11]

With this background of wisdom in mind, we can better understand why Kelsey explains that "This wisdom reaches expression through . . . the myth, the dream, and associated phenomena." I would assert that God-talk is clearly one of these "phenomena." Kelsey goes on to note that "myth has its own way with facts" and that it has a "spontaneous quality about it." We have seen that God-talk does indeed view the facts of an experience in a different way, and this way should be seen as the nonrational, spiritual view of the event. This alternate interpretation does not mean that it is wrong. In our either/or world, we tend to relegate important matters into far too simple dichotomies that may be convenient for us but that are too limiting for the object we have categorized. Myth is just a different way to describe an event that can also be described historically, poetically, scientifically, or musically, in narrative or in art.[12]

An example of how we live with various interpretations of a single event is the morning sunrise. When we get up in the morning, what do we see if we look to the east? All would most likely agree that we see a "sunrise." When we examine this term, we see myth everywhere. Does an inanimate object really "rise"? Perhaps a sun god rises in the morning, but does a nuclear phenomenon in the universe rise? In our scientific world, what we really "see" in the morning is the effect of the earth turning on its axis. This is the rational explanation for what we see, and the proper scientific phrase for what we witness in the morning is "the visual effect of the earth turning on its axis."

But notice that while this explanation is scientifically and rationally correct, it does not adequately "explain" what we really see. We "see" the sun rise, not the earth turning on its axis. While we understand the scientific explanation of what we are seeing, we describe this phenomenon in terms that are really mythical because it is more realistic to us. This explanation demonstrates that, while we claim to be rational, we often unknowingly participate in the realm of myth anyway. This observation goes along with Kelsey's assertion that myth and history can relate the same event, they just do so in different ways. Kelsey then turns this concept around by noting that "myth is a pattern of reality which can be expressed either in human imagination or in history."[13]

We can recall that much of our history has been questioned as to its historical value. Critics have pointed out that what we term objective history is often an interpreted history. This would imply that the imagination has been at work in the collection, evaluation, interpretation, and even writing of the events in question. If this is so, and this is what Kelsey is implying here, then his assertion that myth is history stands on firm ground.[14]

My explorations of God-talk began when I noted that parishioners often revealed one theology in everyday life and then resorted to another when caught in the confusion of crisis. When asked about the discrepancy they often were not aware of any at all. Kelsey addresses this paradox also when he notes that most people are not very consistent in their perceptions of the world. They view experiences with both a head and a heart, to use Kelsey's terms. He means here that people can have both a rational and irrational interpretation of the same event. For example, we all want to believe that God is a loving deity and would never let anything happen to us. In our God-talk, as we have seen in the previous chapters, we often implicate God in the very evil that surrounds us. Thus, our head, that is our reason, tells us one thing about God but our heart, faced with the very real crisis in front of us, may in fact interpret the event in totally different ways. Here we see myth and reason, story and history, paradoxically intertwined.

One of the questions ancients asked of themselves is very familiar to us today: Why should *this* person die at *this* moment? A catastrophic event such as death, for ancient civilizations, would be experienced in its totality and not analyzed and then tossed away intellectually as we do today. In fact, the ancients were quite content with having two conflicting ideas of death exist side by side: (1) Death is simply a part of life, and (2) death is willed or caused to happen by the gods. The tension between the two was simply a fact of life in the ancient Near East, and the one pondering the dilemma had no trouble with the ambiguity.[15]

In our learned society today, however, we seek to eliminate such tensions with a rationalistic focus on the first of these two ambiguities. If our reason cannot rid ourselves of this tension, then we either dodge the issue entirely (this is not rational, therefore, it is not worthwhile or correct to discuss it), or we resort to other methods to help us tolerate it, make sense of it, or explain it away. Allan Bloom, in his provocative book *The Closing of the American Mind,* notes that we have sought to rid ourselves of the eternal questions and tensions which used to lead to creative solutions and thought (and wisdom) and have instead learned to "'feel comfortable' with God, love, and even death" with our society's emphasis upon therapy. Martin Marty, in his reflections on tragedy and grief similarly writes that "What a culture gains in therapy it may lose in its grasp of soul."[16] Caregivers may be unwittingly fostering this unhealthy approach to the ambiguities in life through their rationalistic counseling approaches unless their practice seeks to incorporate the ambiguities of life into a creative new outlook on life after tragedy.

We must now break with Kelsey's model because at this point he himself resorts to the very rational argument that he questions. Kelsey insists that the rift between good and evil may be bridged by believing in the Christ myth. Christ has defeated the power of evil forever and Christians can, in the presence of evil, take refuge in this myth to guide them back to their initial perception that God is indeed all-loving. In suggesting this, Kelsey, like many in our society described previously, wants to remove God from all wrong in our world. Thus, he commits the very sin Erich Zenger attempts to alleviate. Zenger notes that all too often Christian theologians want to disassociate God from evil of any kind. They resort to a Christianizing of the

Old Testament God into a good deity and delegate evil to something other than God.[17] As we have seen, God-talk supports Zenger's assertions that God is involved in both the weal and woe, that is, the Good and Evil, of Creation.[18]

We, of course, know what Kelsey is implying. Those who believe in the Christ myth can conquer evil and the power that death holds over them. Kelsey, however, still does not allow for God to be involved in such evil, because he is investigating a particular problem of evil and its vicious hold on people. Because some have deliberately chosen to pursue evil, they have consciously chosen to separate themselves from God; thus, the very real break in their thinking. We should keep in mind that Kelsey allowed for "lesser" evil to actually be part of God's overall plan that leads to good, which takes us back to our initial assertions about tragedy, suffering, and crisis. God is indeed loving, but using the categories of Kelsey, what is good may indeed appear evil to us initially and, what is evil may eventually work for the good. These are the parameters with which we are engaged in this study.

An important side note may be overlooked in Kelsey's work when he suggests that most religious systems have rituals that allow parishioners to come to grips with evil. He does not enumerate except to suggest that the Catholic practice of confession allows for this discussion and that the Pentecostal emphasis on trials and testing also helps in addressing evil. We will see in the next chapter that one of the reasons why people resort to apocalyptic God-talk is because our current religious rituals as seen in worship do not foster any relevant encounters with evil nor do they allow for any reaction to evil. Churches must address this issue, and Kelsey has hit upon two very important rituals that we should bring back into our churches. Liberal churches have long ignored the testimony time as too emotional, but we can see here the confessional and pastoral needs it addresses. Perhaps the reason why many of the growing mega-churches and churches based on the Willow Creek seeker service model are succeeding, not to mention the more traditional charismatic churches and the evangelical denominations, is because they allow for testimonials in their worship services and because during these services people can address the capricious side of God and do so in a way that employs God-talk without fear of correction as occurs in a more "proper" worship context.

Along with this, Kelsey, like others who have addressed tragedy, relates that suffering must be endured and can be accomplished if suffering is seen as sacrifice. This is exactly what Peter and Paul taught in their writings to fellow sufferers. Again, in our churches today, we have effectively removed any thought of sacrifice from our pop-psychology preaching and spirituality-lite disciplines. This opens the door to today's cultural standard that suffering of any kind is a sign of personal problems.

AN EXPLORATION OF MYTH

We have seen that God-talk certainly appears to be the same as myth. An examination of the definitions of myth reveals that God-talk fits easily within the definitions of myth. According to the *Encyclopedia of Religion*, "myth" is derived from the Greek word *muthos* which means "word" or "speech" as opposed to *logos* which implies "word" in the sense of a reasoned argument. This information fits precisely into Kelsey's pastoral description of the phenomenon. Myth is a story while logos is well-thought-out reason. Myth, according to the *Encyclopedia*, is "an expression of the sacred in words: it reports realities and events from the origins of the world that remain valid for the basis and purpose of all there is . . . [and] functions as a model for human activity, society, wisdom and knowledge." Here again we see that Kelsey's pastoral analysis accurately depicts the realm of myth. As we have seen above, myth explains what cannot be described adequately in rational terms.

Continuing our discussion of the definition of myth, the *Encyclopedia of Religion* notes that it also "occurs side by side with rituals and symbols." Myths, rituals, and symbols will always occur together, but different societies will normally place more emphasis on one of the three. We have already noted that Christian tradition tends to focus on worship (ritual) to the detriment of symbol and myth. We will see later in our discussion of apocalyptic that this genre of religious writing arose when the religious rituals failed to allow for an accurate depiction of the realities surrounding the Israelites. Recall Kelsey's comment that Christians today have neglected important rituals that allowed for the use of myth in religious traditions. It would seem that our society has done its best to squelch myth from its religious rituals. The consequence, as noted previously, is that we have made God into an image of our society.

Myths are told in archaic speech, according to Kees W. Bolle in the *Encyclopedia of Religion*. They attempt to explain the unexplainable. Myth "liberates us from the anxieties . . . of life."[19] Since God-talk erupts mainly during the times of crisis, times of the "unexplainable," it would certainly appear that it comes about in order to relieve anxieties brought about by these very difficult times. From this detailed definition, we see many similarities between myth and the phenomenon of God-talk.

In *Myth and Reality* Mircea Eliade breaks down myths into their various characteristics and roles in society.[20] The characteristics of myth given by Eliade are summarized as follows:

1. Myth constitutes the History of the acts of the Supernaturals.
2. This History is considered to be absolutely true (because it is concerned with realities) and sacred (because it is the work of the Supernaturals).
3. Myth is always related to a "creation," and it tells how something came into existence.
4. By knowing the myth one knows the "origins" of things and thus can control and manipulate the present; this knowledge is experienced ritually either by recounting the myth or by performing the ritual.
5. In one way or another, one "lives" the myth as if one is seized by the sacred, exalting power of the of the events re-enacted.

At first, this list of characteristics seems too abstract for practical use in pastoral ministry, but when compared to the use of God-talk in the pastoral context these characteristics begin to make sense. For example, God-talk constitutes the history of God's acts in the world when it proclaims that "God has taken little Susie." Today we may not believe in such a statement, but in times long ago, the God who created life and death, weal and woe, certainly gave birth to and then took life from people on earth. Our God-talk today keeps vestiges of this belief intact when parents of a newborn child say, "Look at this precious little gift God has given us." We can look to the ancient stories in the Bible for further proof. The phrase "ashes to ashes and dust to dust" that ministers ritually intone during funerals also evokes the ancient myth that told of the "creation" or origin of death (Genesis 3:19).

The truth of God-talk comes alive because it reveals that God is very much involved in every day life. God-talk reveals to the sufferer that, using Eliade's mythical definition, this real crisis is a product of the whims of the supernaturals who have appeared in the guise of Death, Cancer, Evil, Alcoholism, or even The Institution, The Negligent Doctor, or The Bureaucracy. God-talk, as myth, takes the person back to a time of creation. When God created humans, God also limited their days. Death was introduced in the creation stories in the Bible. When someone says that God took Uncle Harry, they are simply evoking the ancient time when God indeed controlled death.

Knowledge of the created acts of the Supernaturals is experienced ritually either by recounting the myth or by performing the ritual. God-talk does both. I have argued that God-talk ritually arises in the time of crisis. When I questioned the claims of the God-talk of my church members after a tragedy was over they reverted to their "usual" theology which often seemed the very opposite of what their God-talk implied. Eliade shows that the ritual use of myth comes in order to invoke the time of the gods and to bring that ancient power back to the present. To maintain some semblance of control over the present situation, the myth is recalled in hope of manipulating the death or present tragedy. We see this enacted in the simple ritual of saying "God bless you" after someone sneezes. We have enacted an ancient ritual that called for God's power to overcome the evil spirits within the person who just sneezed. God blessed creation in times primeval. The invocation of this ancient blessing into the present evil of the sneezing spirits implies that God will rebless this person whose body has been overcome by evil spirits that once were contained in the initial creation.

By recalling or reenacting an ancient myth, the one caught in the crisis can then relive the myth and become "seized by the sacred, exalting power" of the recalled events. What more could someone caught in the throes of chaos want than to be empowered by the initial creative power of the God who, long ago, quelled the destructive forces of chaos?[21]

Thus, Eliade's characteristics fit with many of the forms of God-talk that we encounter in everyday pastoral ministry. Interestingly, Eliade points out that these myths are often taught to initiates during a liminal time of initiation. This sacred time away from the profane time of everyday life resembles the liminal time when crisis grips a person's life. We have already suggested in a previous chapter that the passing on of God-talk comes at such a liminal time. For example, recall the three-day liminal period we usually allot for the funeral process. Regular time seems to stand still while this heightened time of religious significance takes over. God-talk abounds during this period of religious life. Martin Marty describes the wintry time of the soul as a liminal time. Those from the Christian tradition would call this a transfer from *chronos,* that is, linear time, to *kairos,* a spiritual, cyclical time. It is a time for spiritual revelations and deep introspection to sort out what the gods are doing or have done for us. For example, Madeleine L'Engle's reflections during her recovery from a car crash are a literary *kairos* of her liminal convalescence. Eliade notes that it is during such sacred times that the myths are passed on to others. Indeed, in primitive societies, this is the only time the sacred myths can be taught.[22] Since the extensive use of God-talk occurs mostly during the time of the crisis this demonstrates that the time of crisis is indeed a liminal, *kairos* time when the sacred myths, in the form of God-talk, are passed on to the "initiates" who are new to the grief process.

Likewise, Eliade points out that these myths come at a time of creation. He suggests that all myths tie into a time of origins, that is, a time of creation. For example, death is a time of creation in that the sufferers are entering a period of re-creation into a new life without their loved one.[23] Thus, the God-talk invoked during this time is simply a way to recall the ancient creation stories that told of the origins of things, like death, suffering, toil, and new life. This invocation connects the suffering family to the energizing power of the initial creation. This process provides the necessary cosmic, spiritual power to get the sufferers through the present eruption of chaos. We find similar explanations in books on grief that consistently point out that the sufferer must move through a time of death, burial, and resurrection in order to be reborn, that is, recreated, into a life that is new in regard to the past tragedy.

There is one more similarity between ancient societies and our modern world concerning God-talk as myth. Eliade notes that in some situations, dancers, singers, or ritual cantors gather around the person in a time of "new beginning" and intone the myths until the process or situation is over. This sustained ritual surrounds the person with the power of the myth. We can see this phenomenon enacted in our pastoral contexts as well. Recall how family, church members, friends, and other well-wishers gather around those in crisis and begin to perpetuate the God-talk myths. According to Eliade's theory this gathering resembles sacred liturgists who intone the sacred myths to invoke the ancient re-creative powers to come and empower the sufferer through the crisis. In many ways our modern rituals during times of crisis simply perpetuate ancient religious practices.[24]

This brief overview of the characteristics of myth and a comparison to pastoral care contexts reveals that the God-talk we encounter serves an important religious function for the sufferers. It ties them to the ancient creation stories which empowers them to endure the crisis and recreates them for their new beginning after the present crisis. The question for caregivers is: *How* does myth do this? Eliade's observations will help us to understand how this process works.

Eliade emphasizes throughout *Myth and Reality* again and again the role of storytelling. Indeed, this is a ritual that permeates ancient societies and fulfills an important function in their religious life. Myth ties into the unconscious which, for Eliade, is the only part of our person that can fully understand the cosmic dimensions of life.[25] From this point, Eliade compares psychoanalysis to ancient rituals; indeed, many of Eliade's examples of ritual and meditation resemble the dynamics of the counseling session. Both seek to connect the individual with a time of origin either through ancient myths or through childhood stories. Such myths or childhood stories hint of a time long ago when things were good before they became bad in the present. They follow the same pattern.[26]

The similarities between psychoanalysis and ancient rituals are very close. Thus, we should note the importance of incorporating myth into our counseling and understand that what we encounter in our counseling is indeed mythical in many ways. Incorporating biblical stories into the childhood stories part of the counseling process would be a unique way to incorporate myths back into psycho-spiritual healing. For example, ancient initiation rituals often physically mimicked the womb experience of the initiate, as in an initiation period in a cave. Hero stories that depicted the hero or heroine dying and coming back to life also imitate the entrance into the womb of darkness and the re-emergence into the light of new life. A pastoral parallel would be the biblical story of Jonah or the resurrection story of Jesus. Thus, incorporating appropriate scripture stories into the counseling session would replicate for the liminal sufferer ancient ceremonies that mimicked the emergence from the womb into a new life.

A model for using scripture in pastoral counseling has been proposed by Edward P. Wimberly in *Using Scripture in Pastoral Counseling*. He notes that in the counseling session, a "contagious" process of imagination and creativity arises as the counselor and the counselee interact. This process leads to the recalling of stories. Within this process, biblical stories may be cited. Pastoral counselors need to trust this process as they work with their clients. Wimberly points out that in this process a myth arises that symbolizes the problem for the client. The pastoral process seeks to identify this myth and then remythologize the client to move forward from the present interpretive crisis. Wimberly notes that Bible stories can be incorporated into the sessions to "facilitate the discernment" process. Thus, the Bible stories—myths—can help in the healing process.[27]

We can see from this use of scripture that the repetition of ancient myths as depicted in God-talk can be continued and expanded in the counseling session. This ritual serves two purposes. First, it takes the sufferer back to the point of origins and connects the person to the God who "causes" such cosmic occurrences which helps the person to spiritually and psychologically gain control of the situation. Control comes in a spiritually creative leap of acknowledgment that what is happening to them has already happened to others; thus, it is not new. This revelation diminishes the frightful aspects of this apparently new experience. "In telling how things were made, myth reveals by whom and why they were made and under what circumstances," Eliade reminds us. This knowledge helps the sufferer grasp the unknown in the hands of faith and somehow control the chaotic moment. It is the cathartic acceptance of this myth that leads to the new life based on a deeper understanding of "reality, truth and significance."[28]

The God-talk myth forces the sufferer to confront the reality that God the Creator is somehow involved in the present tragedy. The God-talk myth takes the sufferer back to the primordial days when chaos occasionally erupted and had to be contained by the deity. The forgotten deity is brought back to the mind of the sufferer both by the storms of life and the myths that tell of the ancient creating and quelling of such storms. The sufferer must then confront reality and accept it if he or she is to control (bring to closure?) the present episode. This acceptance leads the sufferer to a higher plane of religious understanding since he or she has been taken back to primitive time and allowed to participate in the Cosmic Forces that once tamed Chaos. This experience leads to a new wisdom that will eventually be passed on to other sufferers when they enter the liminal time of tragedy and crisis.

THE BIBLICAL CREATION MYTH

We can see the previous argument carried over into the Bible by examining the two creation stories in Genesis 1-3. The priestly creation story in Genesis 1 comes from a period in Israel's life when death, devastation, and chaos were rampant. After the destruction of Jerusalem and the deportation of the Israelites to Babylon in 587 B.C.E., the people of Israel began looking for answers to their exilic plight. One response offered in Isaiah 53 held that it was God's will to afflict the nation with destruction and exile. Similar thoughts were expressed by the prophet Ezekiel during this time. Another later response was to insist on a strict legal code to atone for the nation's sins. After the exiles returned to Jerusalem in 538 B.C.E., the priests began inaugurating a legal system which, if obeyed, was to keep Israel pure and thus free from any further destructive judgment. Such laws of purity as found in Leviticus were the products of the same hands that produced the Creation in the first chapter of Genesis.[29] But why were these responses suggested? On what did they stand?

The Creation myth in Genesis 1 focused on the ordering of the world by the words (commands? laws?) of one God and countered the prevailing myths of the surrounding countries which described creation as a battle between several gods. Since only one God, the God of Israel, was the Creator, then all happened at the Creator's discretion. Good and evil were both part of God's created order since, unlike the Babylonian's creation myths, good gods were opposed by bad gods on a regular basis. Now there was no other deity to oppose God. God was in control of all Creation, for good or ill.

What is important for our purposes here is that this new creation myth arose amid the chaos, destruction, and confusion brought about by the exile. The old creation myth, in which a loving, compassionate God is depicted as one who walks with the creatures, indeed, makes them with divine hands (Genesis 2-3), was now seen to be deficient. Certainly this kind of God would not bring such destruction to Israel. But a god who was more distant and less compassionate would. Thus, the old myth's depiction of the deity was deemed incorrect due to the present reality. It was replaced with the new myth that more realistically described God as distant and cold yet concerned with order and power for the chaos-ridden world.

Old Testament scholar Claus Westermann notes that creation stories "do not stem from intellectual inquiry into the here and now, but from a concern for security in the face of the existing situation."[30] The Creation myth was a form of extended God-talk, that is, a story used to provide stability in the face of uncertainty.

We may understand the importance of this theological change manifest in the Creation story in another way as well. Leo G. Purdue argues that Creation, not salvation history or covenant and law, is the basis of wisdom texts in the Old Testament.[31] Much of our theology is based on the Old Testament concepts of covenant and law and these are just two ways that tragedy can be interpreted. The metaphor of creation, however, symbolizes a new event in Israel's life. Second Isaiah, which came from the time of Israel's grief as lived out in the exile, is filled with Creation imagery. The Psalms likewise are filled with Creation imagery and the wisdom literature abounds in creation metaphors. But when tragedy falls upon someone, we generally fall back upon salvation and covenant, law and grace, in order to deal with the tragedy. Phrases such as "God will get us through this" and "When this is over I'll get my heart right with God" depict these two theological traditions. What of re-creation? Some may argue that surviving tragedy involves surviving by the grace of God through tragedy or changing one's life around, but the act of re-creating one's life involves much more than just getting through the tragedy and a well-intended desire to do good (in order to keep evil from happening again!). The pain of re-creation is simply more difficult to incorporate into the pastoral conversation. Thus, we dodge it by resorting to the familiar salvation and covenant motifs.

Since wisdom literature abounds with Creation metaphors we have to wonder if that is why ministers do not resort to it when consoling sufferers. The plight of Job is perfect for comparisons with the plight of the sufferer, but how many of us know it well, and correctly enough to incorporate it into the pastoral conversation?

The wisdom literature offers a view on life that goes beyond salvation and law. Because it offers critical observations based on experience rather than being informed by history and theology, it transcends ordinary religious doctrine and reaches into the spiritual realm. God-talk, viewed as wisdom, helps the sufferer to make sense of the crisis in terms that extend far beyond the usual categories of salvation and law.

God-talk fits the definitions of myth. It takes the believer back to a primeval time when God was creating the world. It gives the believer some sense of control over the present chaos when ritualistically invoked. It breaks the continuing *kronos* and instead allows for the slower *kairos*. God-talk, when viewed as myth that arises out of the chaos of crisis, can thus be seen as a way to bring order to a confusing situation. The God-talk we encounter in the pastoral situation is a mythic creation of wise proportions that seeks to counter previous myths that no longer adequately explain or even contain the current crisis.

Chapter 5

God-Talk and Apocalyptic

Intense, eschatological phrases often indicate that people feel threatened and isolated by powers and principalities too vast to be handled or even labeled in a personal way. The caregiver may be caught off guard or intimidated by such God-talk, perhaps even frightened. We may interpret such outbursts as threatening and may immediately feel defensive. On the other hand, we may brush these phrases off as just ignorant superstitions or signs of illiterate religion. But when caregivers examine and interpret these words from the perspective of apocalyptic language, they take on different connotations.

The very mention of the term "apocalyptic" may bring to the mind of a caregiver a flurry of images. Often apocalyptic-thinking people are immediately lumped into a type of blue-collar, second-class believer by academically trained ministers. Even if we are able to dodge this reaction professionally, we still may not know what to do with such antagonistic outbursts from sufferers. Do they intend harm or are they merely invoking a higher power to help them face off unseen powers? If they are invocations of higher powers, what do we make of such words? Understanding the phenomenon of apocalyptic language will help us better interpret this kind of God-talk, and, thus, will help us better care for those who think in such terms in times of grief and tragedy.

WHAT IS APOCALYPTIC?

Much of what we encounter in the emergency room, at the funeral home, at the accident scene, or at the home of a parishioner falls within the same rubric as apocalyptic literature. Standard definitions of apocalyptic imagery help us to identify the parameters of God-talk that seem apocalyptic in scope.[1] Apocalyptic imagery is dualistic, focusing on two ages, this age and the one to come. The dualism entails two opposing powers, such as God and Satan, but the powers can also be described in the guise of kingdoms or other images such as Good and Evil, or, in an ethical dualism such as Justice and Judgment. There is a strong belief in determinism, the notion that all is planned and that Something is at work beyond us in our lives. Along with this determinism comes a kind of secrecy motif, as if the believer knows something that the rest of the world does not. The secret may be revealed to a select few or it will unfold in a later, eschatological time. Apocalyptic imagery often involves demons and angels who work for or against people in everyday struggles, often causing harm or preventing harm from happening. Those who use apocalyptic imagery in their religious language trust in a final judgment and lean toward an eschatological end of events. Often their language is filled with cosmological imagery and they become preoccupied with numbers.

In addition, there is an emphasis on divine retribution in visions of fantastic imagery and cataclysmic battle scenes. An us-them dichotomy is embedded in apocalyptic language that is stark and will not tolerate any ambiguous gray matter. Users of apocalyptic imagery believe in a final day of judgment much like that found in the Old Testament prophets and in the New Testament Book of Revelation. After this time of judgment will come a Golden age of peace and pain-free living. Similes and metaphors, the very stuff of poetry, and prophecy are found lumped together in an apparent irrational manner in apocalyptic imagery. These images often lend themselves to mythological interpretations that sometimes may even incorporate imagery from competing religious traditions. There is an ethical sense to apocalyptic in which God will rain justice upon the earth, resolve matters of injustice, and provide restitution to those who have been wronged by systems, powers, and evil.

God-talk that appears to be apocalyptic may come not only from the sufferer but from those who try to console. These well-wishers may talk in ethereal ways of cosmic matters that seem mythical or fantastic. They may look back through past years and begin to relate patterns they have seen, whether they are apparent to others or not, and talk as if someone was revealing to them a long line of predetermined events that are leading a world-ending catastrophe. While such talk may appear bothersome to the caregiver, we should learn to see it through the eyes of apocalyptic where it comes as a way to provide hope in the time of greatest tribulation.

D. S. Russell addresses what may be a concern for caregivers when attempting to interpret apocalyptic imagery used by clients and parishioners. Some caregivers will no doubt think that apocalyptic imagery is an escape from reality. Indeed, with all of the mythology, the emphasis on another world, and an insistence on justice coming "one day," this would seem true. But Russell notes that much apocalyptic literature in ancient times dealt with how to live life in the present while in the presence of evil and unexplained suffering.[2]

Sociologist Tex Sample, who investigates "hard-living people," confronted this issue. He, too, thought the offensive, apocalyptic vocabulary was an evasive escape from reality. But on further investigation, he discovered that it was an important tool for dealing with the present chaotic reality.[3] John J. Collins demonstrates this further and more pointedly for caregivers when he explains that the use of apocalyptic imagery helps the sufferer to transcend death rather than escape it. He notes that apocalyptic, while often equated with eschatology, is not fixated just on the end times. "If the apocalyptic books were written, as is widely believed, to give hope to the faithful in times of oppression, it would be indeed extraordinary if they were primarily concerned with 'the end' and not with what lies beyond it." It was not the end times so much as the hope that lay in the future beyond the end that sustained believers through their particular persecutions. Through the fantastic imagery and the cosmic mythologies of apocalyptic literature, "the restrictions of the human condition are cast off and in particular death is transcended." Collins concludes that "present experience and future hope were intrinsically connected and mutually interdependent" in the eyes of apocalyptic thinkers.[4] This "future expectation" in apocalyptic helps the sufferer endure the present oppression or tragedy. In other words, it is not an escape mechanism at all but a complete faith system worked out in fantastic imagery that provides a present hope in a hopeless present. This hope bolsters the sufferer through the current crisis until a sense of normalcy comes back to his or her world.

From a theological perspective, the problem for caregivers lies in the approach taken to the crisis. Jurgen Moltmann argues that our theology has been centered around Greek philosophies concerning the proof of God. Such proofs are based on natural theology arguments, yet Moltmann concludes that they demean the idea of revelation, because such arguments threaten the very content of revelation. "The essential difference here is accordingly not between the so-called nature gods and a God of revelation, but between the God of the promise and the gods of the epiphanies." Moltmann believes theologians, ministers, and caregivers are so influenced by the God of the epiphanies in the biblical story that we cannot see the real God of the Promise. In other words, the epiphanies are simply part of the greater drama of the ever-unfolding Promise. We have, in effect, placed the historical cart before the eschatological horse. Thus, according to Moltmann, eschatology, not theological proofs of God, should be the real focus of pastoral caregivers. This eschatology is the provider of hope to those in crisis. Pastoral care based on theological proofs of God and centered on the epiphanies of scripture (such as the exodus, the commandments at Sinai, etc.), neglect the overarching theme of Promise that informs and interprets these events.[5]

WHERE DOES APOCALYPTIC COME FROM?

The scholarly debate surrounding the origins of apocalyptic is much in question at this time, but this flux is informative for caregivers in that many of the issues have counterparts in the area of pastoral care.

Apocalyptic literature initially arose during times of political, economic, and religious instability in the ancient Near East, possibly beginning during the time of Ezekiel and continuing into the Christian Era. It arose as a "response of faith" and eventually turned into a "literature of the oppressed who saw no hope."[6] In New Testament times, however, it was perpetuated because of intense persecution by the government and religious leaders upon the fledgling Christian believers.[7]

Already we can see some parallels for pastoral care. People caught in the unseen yet real arms of government oppression, hospital red tape, HMO negligence, or economic chaos certainly see no hope in their present crisis. Faced with such large and evasive adversaries, they have little recourse but to turn to fantastic language to capture this evil enemy and reduce it to a tolerable foe. Those fighting such formidable enemies certainly feel persecuted and very much alone, just as the ancient Jews and early Christians did centuries ago.

But social, political, and economic woes were not the only sparks of apocalyptic flames. Russell notes that there were reasons within Israel's and early Christendom's own religious systems, such as deficiencies within the worship cult, that led to the creation of a new religious language for the suffering Israelites. For instance, the decline of prophecy during and after the exile led to a rise of the prominence of law. This change in religious institutions indicates a break between oral religion and scribal religion. During this time, literate religion pushed aside oral, "illiterate," faith. The cold practices of legalism took over from the passionate vociferousness of pastoral prophecy. While prophecy critiqued worship practices, providing a check against dispassionate ritual that led to social and religious corruption during the pre-exilic monarchy, the shift to a legalistic emphasis focused more on the critique of personal behavior. The result was that the worship cult failed to address and give voice to the real pastoral needs of the people.

With the demise of prophecy and its blazing checks against the external powers of politics and social changes, however, no other manner of critical religious expression developed until apocalyptic literature arose. While deriving from prophecy, apocalyptic discourse was perpetuated in literary rather than oral form, thus providing an acceptable counterpart to the written laws of Judaism. In essence, Rabbinic legalism and Jewish apocalyptic were two sides of the same religious coin used to tender the stresses and strains of everyday trials and tribulations.[8]

Taking this thought further, Jon D. Levenson concludes that apocalyptic literature came about to address the disjunction between the ideal world as expressed in the temple liturgy and the real world as experienced in the suffering of innocent people. By recalling the ancient battles between God and Chaos, as manifested in various mythical personae in apocalyptic literature, the apocalyptic reader hoped to provoke God once again to tackle the evil that surrounded his or her world.[9]

We can certainly relate this information to our own efforts in caregiving. Levenson's conclusion provides a model for us to see how the apocalyptic phenomenon can fill a religious void in the life of the sufferer. People caught in grief, oppression, and tragedy find themselves temporarily in the wilderness between the God who conquered evil and the reality that evil is still able to get loose and wreak havoc in our lives. Levenson demonstrates well that a flawed belief system based on Genesis 1 and the theological understanding of *creation ex nihilo* led to this mistaken belief that God has defeated evil forever. Using other biblical texts, however, he demonstrates that God throughout the Bible is constantly plagued by evil that breaks loose periodically, either because God seems to turn the other way occasionally, thus allowing Chaos to escape from its underground prison, or because, as Job 41 reveals, God simply likes to play or sport with the evil Leviathan. It is this "play" which is manifested on earth as evil, catastrophe, or injustice. Levenson's argument explains why sufferers often complain that it seems as if God is toying with them. In their own God-talk way, they are voicing the mythical theology that Levenson describes!

Exploring Levenson's argument demonstrates why many in the field of pastoral care may choose to deny his claim. The theology that chaos erupts because God has turned the other way, fallen asleep, or simply needs a sparring partner goes against the grain of our current popular theology that God is good and only does good deeds. Yet if we look behind such God-talk phrases as "Has God forgotten me?" or "Is God ever going to look favorably on me?" we can see that many sufferers unwittingly verify what Levenson suggests. The thought that God would fall asleep on the job or even cause tragedy just to have fun at our expense is not a comforting one, yet our God-talk often suggests that, deep within our soul, we believe God acts this way.

While the rosy, idealistic temple liturgy, depicting God as one who has things well in hand, was, and still is, the dominant theological underpinning of our interpretation of suffering, those caught in the everyday bumps and bruises of life's realities often find it lacking. Cast in the dubious role of Job, who even maintained religious rituals for his family, such faithful believers follow the law and worship God in hope that ritual observance will ensure a life free of hardship. Betrayed by this belief and its rituals, however, sufferers realize the inadequacy of this belief system in the face of tragedy and oppression. Some turn to yet even more stringent legalism, as manifest in many a confession voiced to caregivers. ("I'm going to turn my life around this time. No more drinking.")

Others, however, employ the imagery of apocalyptic to solve this chaotic riddle. Their apocalyptic imagery incorporates an ancient combat motif to remind, indeed, provoke a seemingly lazy, complacent or distracted God to once more contain the forces of Evil. In essence, what the ritualistic language and worship cultus fails to interpret, the apocalyptic literature and imagery explains in quite adequate terms. Caregivers need to understand that, in times of grief and crisis, some people will shift their language similarly. In essence, apocalyptic imagery preserves the mystery of God while satisfying the longing for divine explanations.

One way to picture this use of apocalyptic is to see it as *re-mythologizing* the typical myths as depicted in the temple ritual.[10] Counselors are no strangers to this technique of re-mythologizing or rethinking images disclosed during the counseling session, and Donald Capps' method of reframing is informative for our discussion.[11] Often the crisis as presented to the minister or caregiver is really a crisis of competing theologies. When suffering is encountered, to use the reframing method, the sufferer voices confusion at how a loving God could do such things to good people. The usual response from the pastoral caregiver would be to retain the loving God image and work within this image. Thus, issues of theodicy and the problem of evil ensue. In reframing, however, rather than working with the loving God image, the counselor would instead counter with an instinctual reframing and suggest that maybe God is not so good after all. This reframing of the event then allows the sufferer to see that perhaps his or her image of God is indeed the problem behind the spiritual confusion.

The present experience of tragedy brings a different side of God to the sufferer's attention, one that does not compute with past and heretofore functional theologies. To take Job as an example again, such theologies are based on the premise that God is good and just and thus if we are good and just and religiously punctual with our cultic rituals, then we are assured a good life. This is the premise behind the God-talk "I was a good person. I went to church, taught Sunday school. Why is this happening to me?"

With the present tragedy, however, the counselor must now guide the client to rethink or re-mythologize his or her images of God in order to comprehend the present crisis. Again, to use Job as an example, he had to reorganize his theology to accommodate the fact that God could indeed send tragedy his way, thus calling into question his God-is-just functional theology.

In apocalyptic literature, God is not so good. God destroys, causes suffering, brings on plagues, and interrupts the heavens. And these tribulations are rained upon the good and the bad. But the reader of apocalyptic understands that such a devastating God does so *in order that* good may eventually triumph. Thus, one purpose of apocalyptic language is to reframe the "good" God revered in weekly worship rituals into the picture of present suffering.

Another purpose of apocalyptic imagery is to provoke God to wake up to the present tragic reality and do something about it. The use of apocalyptic imagery in God-talk by the sufferer may simply be an intentional or even unconscious way to call upon God to turn back to matters at hand and check the disastrous forces that are playing havoc with the creatures of earth. It may also be a tacit admission that God is at work in the tragedy since the apocalyptic mind-set believes God is ultimately in control of all things, including evil on earth.[12]

Such uses and writing of apocalyptic literature reveal anything but an ignorant or even illiterate side to apocalyptic imagery. Indeed, many scholars have noted the profundity of apocalyptic literature and its purpose and have proposed that apocalyptic may have roots in Israel's wisdom tradition.[13] Jonathan Z. Smith finds that this tradition arose from priests trained in astronomy, astrology, mathematics, historiography, and ancient lore.[14] The priests from this learned tradition "developed complex hermeneutic and exegetic techniques to bridge the gap between paradigm and particular instance, between past and present." Ancient texts were "updated" to apply to the present predicament. This process included glosses, interpretation and reinterpretation, even to the extent of fabrication of ancient precedents and archetypes.

Again we must note the way apocalyptic images are put together in a willy-nilly fashion out of ancient theologies, stories, and history in order to address the current crisis situation. The cross cultural, folk-type style of apocalyptic, while defying reason and logic, is simply a diverse yet wise, indeed, innovative way to put some sense of order to a very disordered world that cannot be cleaned up with normal, "acceptable" theologies.

Apocalyptic imagery encountered in the pastoral context may likewise seem a hodgepodge of confused theology, religious, and even denominational traditions and superstitious beliefs. It is up to the caregiver to determine whether the sufferer is spiritually or psychologically confused. And this assessment underscores the very importance of understanding the imagery and the use of apocalyptic in a pastoral setting.

THE BIAS AGAINST APOCALYPTIC LANGUAGE

Paul Hanson notes that there have been periods in intellectual history when apocalyptic literature has been rejected by refined, rational minds and his discussion helps caregivers understand how a bias might be present when apocalyptic God-talk is confronted. He points to the period before World War I as just such a time. "For the intelligentsia of the Enlightenment, for the idealistic philosophers and liberal theologians of the nineteenth century, and for sober scholars and thinkers at the beginning of this century, apocalypticism, with few exceptions, was ignored or repudiated with loathing." He then describes how this academic mood changed with the onset of World War I. Caught up in the chaos of the war, people began looking for answers and order. Ancient writings were examined for clues. These writings told of cosmic forces battling for control of the earth. The answers that were sought were found in apocalyptic literature. Indeed, apocalyptic literature seemed more accurately to describe reality as it actually was experienced than did the constructions of the philosophical idealists and the harmonious systems of the liberal theologians. Citing Carl Jung, Hanson notes that real life is filled with extreme opposites such as are found in apocalyptic dualisms: day and night, good and evil, birth and death, joy and pain. He concludes that "ancient Jewish apocalyptic writings grew out of the courage to stare into the abyss on the edge of which an entire civilization tottered, and a willingness to describe what the fantasy of faith enabled the human eye to glimpse beyond the tragedy."[15]

This notion of "fantasy" may disturb the caregiver and produce another bias against apocalyptic imagery and literature. In the world of pastoral care, fantasy brings up connotations of delusions, perhaps even living in a fantasy world as opposed to real life. The very task of caregivers is to lead clients and parishioners from the potentially dysfunctional world of make-believe back into reality. Thus, the confusion that apocalyptic imagery by its very nature presents fantasy may mislead caregivers to dismiss it outright as enabling the sufferer to dodge reality altogether. As we have seen, this is not the case for most of those who voice their confusion in the language of apocalyptic imagery.

Stephen L. Cook also offers insights into the bias against this category of God-talk.[16] He notes that many interpreters of apocalyptic imagery, both professional and academic, lay and clergy, tend to equate apocalyptic language with those on the fringe of society. Such people are often lumped together with those whom we consider troubled psychologically. These inclinations have unfortunately been passed on uncritically to those trained in seminaries through the scholarly works read and studied by students.

Some have considered apocalyptic writings to be the product of sociopolitical fringe groups who write out of their marginalization and after their various defeats at the hand of society or government. We have only to watch the evening news or read the newspapers and magazines to see this enacted before our eyes. For example, when FBI agents surround right-wing apocalyptic "cults" in the middle of a wilderness, this stereotype is further perpetuated.

Cook relates that Julius Wellhausen, one of the most influential Old Testament scholars in early modern biblical studies, concluded apocalypticism was void of any theological value.[17] His conclusion stems from the understanding that apocalyptic thought came from outside of Israelite religious circles. Subsequent biblical scholars, building on the foundation of Wellhausen and others, simply assumed that, because of this outside, Persian influence, apocalyptic was not relevant to proper Israelite religion. This academic bias is simply the case of trying to fit the square pegs of apocalyptic writing, with its irrational and difficult imagery, into the round holes of "normal" (i.e., acceptable) religious thought.

There are modern, pastoral parallels to each of these notions. First, some pastoral caregivers may quickly turn their heads when apocalyptic imagery is presented to them. Such diffidence comes because of a lack of understanding of the social and religious underpinnings of apocalyptic imagery or because caregivers are only acquainted with a basic understanding of biblical imagery for use in pastoral care (salvation, law, grace, sacraments, etc.). When the minister is expected to bring or highlight the presence of God into the pastoral situation it is difficult to envision how an apocalyptic moment can be combined with an empathic statement.

Second, apocalyptic language does seem irrational and is quite illogical because that is its very nature. One reading of the Book of Revelation brings this to mind. Consider Helmut Koester's description of apocalyptic imagery:

> Apocalyptic language prefers associations within a sequence of images to a logical progression of thought; it permits individual features and metaphors to stand side by side without connections rather than composing them into a coherent picture; it repeats traditional materials without commentary and then unexpectedly indicates the direction of a new interpretation through striking omissions or additions. The special views of the author will not always find expression within the various images of the visions, but rather in their order, sequence, and numbers, in comments, and interpolations, interruptions of the context, and hymnic, liturgical, and parenetic additions.[18]

According to this description, there is legitimate cause for concluding that apocalyptic language is irrational, but this raises a question: irrational as compared to what? We could make a legitimate argument that the rational, ideal world of worship, law, and doctrine has left the sufferer lacking for an adequate vocabulary to use in the face of tragedy. Thus, compared to the sufferer's real world, the normal theological system now seems very irrational. In the presence of tragedy, the tables are now turned. The rational is now irrational, thus, what was heretofore perceived as irrational must be quite reasonable.

Likewise, if, as we have seen, apocalyptic language and writings derive from a period of intense suffering, persecution and hopelessness, times that pastoral caregivers know are not conducive to lucid thoughts,[19] then who would expect such babble to make sense? If we examine apocalyptic literature from a pastoral care perspective, we could say that it is an extended form of God-talk delivered in the context of tragedy, and given the irrational circumstances surrounding the situations, we should only expect irrational discourse during these times of storms.

Note that we are talking about irrational talk, not delusional talk. The pastoral caregiver must be familiar enough with apocalyptic imagery to be able to distinguish the difference. Indeed, if we think about the conversation taking place at the funeral home, the home of the suffering family, the emergency room, or the church vestibule during and after a tragedy, we will find a disparate amalgam of religious language taking place. Picture a person who mutters scripture while another makes threats while a small group hums "Amazing Grace" while another laments "Why, O Lord?" This concatenation of images and genres—scripture, history, salvation, assurance, liturgy, hymnody, and prayer, to name just a few examples—when viewed from a distance, bears all the marks of an apocalyptic thriller and presents the caregiver with an overwhelming "book" to read and interpret during the time of crisis. Put all of these examples into the pages of one sufferer as witnessed in several pastoral visits to this person throughout a tragedy, and the picture indeed looks even more irrational. How can one person think and verbalize so many disparate theologies and thoughts? Is it no wonder that caregivers may retreat to familiar theology when confronted with apocalyptic God-talk?

We must realize, however, that hope is not tied to one particular symbol, as John J. Collins points out in his discussion of apocalyptic literature.[20] To the sufferer, whose one ideal of God's presence has been toppled by the present tragedy, the flirtation with myriad images of hope may be the only sustaining factor in her recovery. As Andrew D. Lester points out, hope is a major ingredient in the recovery process yet, sadly, the introduction of hope into the pastoral process has been missing.[21] Allowing the sufferer to fantasize apocalyptically about the present, using images from the past to build a potential future, may be the one link necessary to revitalize the faith of the sufferer.

To help us better understand the apocalyptic mind-set and how it provides a sense of hope for sufferers, we can look to MTV and the Generation X culture for help in how to approach, handle, and interpret this complex phenomenon. In the world of MTV, the viewer is pounded with a barrage of seemingly irrational images fired within the noise of incessant music. The viewer, if not familiar and comfortable with such situations, is overwhelmed and unable to interpret the message. Like many religious folks who do not understand MTV or its adherents, such viewers tend to retreat to familiar theologies and use them to condemn those who live in the virtual world of MTV-land. Those who understand MTV are often relegated to the life of marginality, especially members of Generation X.

Yet, as Tom Beaudoin explains, the MTV generation is very much an apocalyptic people who feel alienated from their society and its religious structures. Caught up in the confusion of their times and forced to deal with oppressive and abusive social, political, and economic woes, they feel exiled to the margins of society. Yet Beaudoin makes a strong case for interpreting their MTV videos in a religious manner. Indeed, the term "apocalyptic" is found throughout his examination of Generation X. One simply must learn to make sense of the erratic, irrational, and illogical string of images in these videos in order to understand and appreciate their religious message.[22]

These conclusions again shed some light in the realm of pastoral care. Those who resort to apocalyptic imagery may not be so much marginal as simply in need of a more effective religious language to express the pain and suffering they are experiencing. For example, most people encounter God through the weekly worship rituals. If we examine these rituals closely, however, pastoral questions arise. How, and when, does one cry out to God or plead for divine retribution in the ritual and calm of Sunday worship? Where is the time of questioning, doubt, rebuke, and even disbelief? Conversely, it is nearly impossible, not to mention whether or not it is feasible, to break into a version of Holy Worship when in the context of the emergency room. Yet, when all one has experienced is liturgical language such as hymnody, lectionary texts, formal prayers, and the doxology, and their limited doctrinal base, this is the only manner remaining with which to express grief, and it is not exactly the most appropriate one. Even normally staid worshipers may find, in the throes of grief, that hymns and prayers, not to mention announcements, simply do not give vent to what they feel and need to express. Having lived a life of law and covenant expressed through weekly worship and daily devotion, they realize that this avenue, while serving a need in the ideal world of everyday normality, does them no good in dealing with the real drama of tragedy.

Thus, they must resort to a different way to express their pain and frustration, not to mention their hope. Voicing prophetic doom to the unseen powers that caused the tragedy may be the only graceful outlet for them at this point in their grief process. Having vented through the voice of apocalyptic language during their time of oppression, tragedy, or persecution, they will, with the proper guidance and understanding, someday return to the calm of the Sunday ritual and settle back into the "normal" theology and the "appropriate" worship patterns. As caregivers, we need to be aware of the various religious languages that may come our way and be prepared to interpret or translate them into appropriate pastoral care and ministry.

HOW APOCALYPTIC WORKS IN PASTORAL CARE

We have seen throughout this discussion that apocalyptic seeks to bridge the gap between the conflict of a past ideal and a present reality. This disparity centers around the storm's eye of ideal religious beliefs that God is in control of Creation and its ever-present Chaos and the reality that, despite these beliefs, Chaos occasionally breaks loose and wreaks havoc on Creation and its creatures. For many, whether the Israelites of the Hebrew Bible or the person crying in front of us, the tension takes place as we try to use "normal" ritualistic words from our church school teachings, liturgies and worship services, and places of regular religious involvement to describe an experience that is anything but normal. Apocalyptic imagery fills this void by giving the sufferer a new and more accurate vocabulary to use in times of crisis.

We can use a more specific example by examining Adele Yarbro Collins' treatment of the Book of Revelation. She writes that this book was written "to overcome the unbearable tension . . . between what was and what ought to have been." This tension is recreated through the use of apocalyptic imagery by the writer so that the reader could relive the tension. The vision from Patmos was written to "overcome the intolerable tension between reality and hopeful faith."[23] The question for caregivers is, How does apocalyptic do this?

Collins describes the tension between what was expected and what was really happening as cognitive dissonance, a term pastoral caregivers are quite familiar with. This is the chaotic state of the mind as it deals with "the great disparity between expectations and reality." Borrowing from French anthropologist Claude Levi-Strauss, Collins notes apocalyptic builds a myth that helps to mediate the contradictions experienced between the unsettling disparities lived by the sufferer. Apocalyptic literature brought forth from the reader the emotions that no doubt lay dormant or unexpressed deep within: fear of the oppression or crisis, aggression toward the seen or unseen powers, resentment toward those who were not suffering, and envy of those who lived life without tragedy. The apocalyptic language creates a "virtual experience" by "manipulating the thoughts, attitudes, and feelings" of its audience. Various narrative techniques such as implied authority, typology, symbols, allegory, and myths are employed by the author and this produces an intensification of the feelings and emotions experienced by the sufferer.

This slow, intense building of powerful emotions comes to a crisis point that Collins and other interpreters of apocalyptic refer to as "catharsis," a term coined by Aristotle that comes from the medical profession yet is also a major ingredient of Greek tragedy. "The emotions of the audience are purged in the sense that their feelings of fear and pity are intensified and given objective expression" through the plot and symbols of the apocalyptic story. "Fearful feelings are vented by the very act of expressing them . . ." in the reading, hearing, or citing of apocalyptic imagery.

In psychological terms, dangerous feelings are given a release by the very act of reading the apocalyptic work. Through the magic of story, with all of its symbols, plot, and energy, the reader is given the conviction that "what ought to be *is*." The fact that a heavenly reality is presented as a future hope soothes the wounds brought about by the present earthly affliction. In effect, "I will be given my due someday." In essence, the apocalyptic story recreates a new world that replaces the old one and helps the sufferer through the present crisis.

There is, of course, a danger here. Some may become too caught up in the recreated reality. Indeed, in her presentation of this information, Collins refers to the schizophrenic individual who lives in such a world. The key for caregivers is to check the energy expended upon this new "reality." If it is used to help the sufferer through the crisis and then referred to less after the crisis, it most likely reveals a beneficial use of apocalyptic imagery.

This catharsis of expectations is no stranger to the pastoral profession. Much of our grief counseling centers on expectations that are unrealistic. "I always thought she would live forever" is the cathartic cry of one whose idealistic expectations have been broken by an eye-opening present reality. Collins notes that apocalyptic language and imagery helps the sufferer to transfer hopes for a better world here to hopes for a better world there. Likewise, aggressions that are experienced here are transferred to something or someone else through the image of apocalyptic. When a sufferer says, "You'll get yours, buddy. Your time is coming!", he may simply be employing the rhetoric of apocalyptic to the perceived enemy, say, the drunk who killed his daughter. In this context, he is saying that he believes that God will vindicate the injustice done to him by this "enemy."

This projection into the cosmic future is standard fare in apocalyptic literature and is yet another way the literature works to lead the sufferer through the present catharsis. Apocalyptic makes it easy for the hearer to gain some distance from the surrounding evil. With this distance, the hearer will gain some control over the evil as well as some detachment from the tragedy.

BIBLICAL IMAGES FOR PASTORAL APOCALYPTIC INTERPRETATION

There are several places in the Bible where we can look for apocalyptic images for use in our pastoral counseling. I will only point out a few here for our discussion. For example, the sufferer who feels punished by God yet who faithfully feels that there is a positive, instructive and thus divine reason for this retribution, may find solace in the pages of Ezekiel. Although the imagery is often bizarre, a consistent pattern of punishment and then grace is found throughout the book that, when reflected upon, may provide a new understanding for the present crisis. Ezekiel explains that God is indeed the cause of Israel's banishment to Babylon yet at the same time God is working on a new start for these hurting people. God will not allow anyone or anything else to harm them. This promise provides comfort in that God, not Evil or Fate, is involved in the lives of the sufferer. Thus, the present crisis is simply one event in the long continuum of promise that God gives to believers.

Ezekiel also provides a pastoral context in which to explore the need for changing theology. The basis for most Old Testament theology is the dictum from Exodus 20:5 that the sins of the parents will be passed on to the third and fourth generation. We see this in much of our therapy and pop-psychology today. Unfortunately, this mind-set and concomitant therapeutic methodology has generated more blame than healing. Ezekiel, aware of the suffering of his people, however, introduced a new theology. Now, he proclaims in 18:4ff., people will pay for their own sins. When seen in the context of reframing, this makes sense. Why spend time blaming others for our pain when we could instead be working on a new paradigm or theology to help us move into the present and future? Along with this, the counselor can use this shift to help the sufferer see how important it is to change theologies in the times of crisis to make better sense of the situation and to move forward in hope and healing.[24]

The Book of Daniel also provides a scenario that may prove helpful to sufferers who feel victimized by various oppressive systems. Daniel tells the wicked King Nebuchadnezzar that he believes God will deliver him from the fiery furnace and that, even though God should decide not to deliver him from this ordeal, he will still believe. Here we see a faith that is resilient against oppressive systems. The story is rich in imagery that should be fruitful for pastoral exploration.

There is the sense, in biblical passages that deal with suffering, that the impending judgment of God—certainly an apocalyptic event—brings about the present suffering experienced by the faithful. 1 Peter 4:12-19 touches upon this subject. Peter is writing to Christians who are suffering. He reminds them that their present afflictions are simply part of the coming judgment. This advice should have come as no surprise to Peter's readers because it was well known that Jesus himself predicted the coming judgment and the rending of family, society, and government (e.g., Mark 13). These texts alone should help us to understand that those who use the apocalyptic mind-set to interpret their present suffering and trials see very clearly that their crisis is simply part of the larger apocalyptic movement of God.

At the same time, the sufferer, using the Book of Revelation as a guide, may feel that Satan, not God, is at work in the trials thrown his or her way. Such imagery is not unusual and may not be confusing at all for the sufferer. But the caregiver needs to remain aware of the imagery throughout the pastoral encounter and make a note if it seems to cause undue stress or psychological problems. These images may simply be useful for the sufferer and may even change after the crisis is over.

The caregiver should not be surprised if some sufferers exhibit joy rather than depression in their trials. Just as Peter advises, some will take joy in this persecution, feeling as though their suffering is part of the very will of God. Just as Jesus suffered, died, and was resurrected as part of God's plan, so they too feel that their present suffering is part of a larger cosmic event that has yet to be revealed to them. This is their hope and, as long as this joy is not a way to deny the pain or the grief, we need to be careful not to interfere with this. At the same time, we need to be on the lookout for this interpretation to become skewed in becoming the cause for dangerous behavior, such as that embodied in cults or militia movements. The caregiver should probe carefully and compassionately should such imagery arise in order to adequately assess what is being said.

On the negative side, one could make an argument that the Book of Daniel encourages religious defiance as part of the apocalyptic belief. When Daniel defies the orders of King Nebuchadnezzar, this action was part of the apocalyptic theme of the book of Daniel. This behavior may be played out negatively, for example, as one takes on the hospital establishment and breaks the rules of critical care units. On the other hand, this behavior may take on positive tones as when the sufferer defies the doctor's orders and refuses treatment, claiming that he is relying on God's help. A miraculous cure may follow, or heartache may ensue. The caregiver must use discernment when confronting such dangerous and confusing situations. It may be helpful to remind the sufferer that both Jesus, while predicting such calamity, and Peter, while pointing out the joy of suffering, never called for violent reactions, and both insisted on allowing God to work out the divine plan in God's time and on God's terms. In true apocalyptic style, only God is allowed to use destruction to further the divine plan. Those of us caught in this plan simply must trust God to work things out.

Apocalyptic God-talk confronted in pastoral conversations can be better understood if caregivers are aware of the dynamics of, the psychology surrounding, and the spiritual need for such imagery. Apocalyptic imagery may reveal an inadequate theology in the soul of the sufferer, and it may indicate that previous religious rituals do not provide proper voice to the tragic interruptions of everyday life and its functional theology. Caregivers need to be aware of personal, professional, and educational biases in their training that might lead to misinterpretation of apocalyptic imagery in the pastoral conversation. Once understood in its proper context, apocalyptic imagery provides caregivers with a unique, cathartic avenue to help the hurting soul interpret tragedy and walk through the valley of the shadow until the dawn of hope brings about a new light for a new day.

Conclusion: Genres of Faith

We have seen that God-talk arises during the times of crisis in a ritualistic, mythic response to the tragedy surrounding the sufferer. It is paradoxical, irrational, and filled with metaphors, similes, and allegories. God-talk conforms to the category of myth and fills an apocalyptic, spiritual need for those caught in the throes of crisis and tragedy. It might be voiced by the educated and illiterate, by those from both high and low church traditions. The use of God-talk allows the sufferer to somehow explain the present tragedy and put it into a graspable perspective. Once the crisis has passed, most sufferers will shy away from God-talk or sometimes even admit that they do not really perceive God as one who does what the God-talk suggests.

We have found throughout this discussion that, when we try to describe God-talk, invariably literary categories are called upon for illumination. Interpreting God-talk from a literary perspective leads us beyond the rational discourse of scientific method and instead takes us into the realm of "what if . . . ?" For example, myth is a literary category and it must be treated as such. Myth is a supra-natural, spiritual, or religious explanation for something that cannot be explained adequately through other methods, such as science. At the same time, however, myth can exist side by side with scientific explanations, as in the ancient Near East, in order to provide a more multifaceted explanation of life's experiences. If sufferers use myth, and apocalyptic for that matter, to explain their crises, they might also use other literary categories as well in their attempts to make sense of their suffering.

Given that we have discussed God-talk through these literary categories we are now in the position to suggest that the soul expresses itself through genres of faith. We have seen a few genres already. As we conclude let us briefly consider three other genres of faith in relation to God-talk.

GOD-TALK AND THE GENRE OF TRAGEDY

We saw in the previous chapter that one of the outcomes of apocalyptic is catharsis and we noted that this emotional state is part of the literary genre of tragedy. A tragedy was written to explain the conflict between a person and a superior force so that pity or terror is evoked among the listeners.

Many forms of God-talk depict the tragic accounts of good people caught up in the bad times of life. Sufferers come to us with such stories looking for comfort and even explanations. It is helpful to realize that similar themes occur throughout the Bible. W. Lee Humphreys has investigated several biblical incidents through the lens of tragedy, and his insights are beneficial to the field of pastoral care.[1]

For example, Joseph had to endure hardships so that God's larger purpose might be carried out (Genesis 45:4ff.). Joseph's many earthly ups and downs, the very stuff of tragedy, were caused by the superior force of God. In the Book of Job, we meet this same fate because, as we have seen repeatedly in this discussion, God is the source of the innocent Job's suffering. The plot lines of these stories manifest the definition of tragedy—a righteous and innocent person must fight against a supernatural force. Tragedy is also seen in the New Testament in the person of Paul, who suffered many afflictions so that the Gospel might be carried out. The epitome of tragedy, of course, is Jesus. His cry from the cross, "My God, my God, why have you forsaken me?" is no doubt in the background of every sufferer's lament.

The similarity between God-talk and the literary genre of tragedy is quite strong. Both relate the plot of the hero who, through the "flaw" of doing good works, meets with some unexpected fate. The tension in the plot of tragedy and in the lament of sufferers centers around the assumption that life is orderly, somehow controlled by a force that is usually divine in some aspect.

Humphreys notes that, in the Hebrew Bible, tragedy arose during times of crisis, both political and religious. In order to answer the existential questions such crises provoke, ancient writers produced the tragic stories that we now read in the Hebrew Bible. Humphreys relates that tragic stories are simply "giving expression to profoundly articulated terrors and hopes of human beings inexorably bound to a nexus of forces that sustain them even as they overpower them."[2]

Again, the parallels between tragedy and God-talk are clear. As we have seen already, the person using God-talk is not one who believes the world operates on its own, with fate and chance striving to prove they have divine powers. Those caught in the throes of tragedy are actually caught between the rock of belief in an ordered world and the hard place of life in its most chaotic form. The tension and the paradox of this predicament are articulated in the tragic God-talk that we hear from sufferers.

The crux of the matter is, simply, "I *thought* God was in control." The sufferer's preconceived perception of the order is not in agreement with the present reality. Thus, tragedy and the similar God-talk are concerned with the reordering of our perceptions of the cosmos. As we begin this restructuring of our life's presuppositions, we ponder thoughts that we have never considered before. *Maybe* God really does take people indiscriminately from this earth. *Maybe* God really does cause war, famine, poverty, and crisis. Through the interpretation of our soul, we are simply trying to reorient our previous perceptions of the world to the current reality. The imaginative avenue of tragedy allows the sufferer to do so through the imagination.

Interestingly, in the classic portrayals of tragedy, according to Aristotle, the hero winds up in the predicament through the flaw of *harmatia*—that is, sin.[3] This fact may cause alarm in many caregivers, but there are several ways to focus on this issue. The easiest would be to note the person dying of emphysema who smoked all his or her life. Or to look at the lax ways of parents who ignored their child only to see the child run over by a car. In these cases, the tragedy was caused by a sin. If we look further, we might also note that there is another sin deep within these scenarios that centers around the person's perception of reality. Simply stated, the "sins" are *mis*perceptions concerning God.

First, we have the misperception, or sin, of "It won't happen to me." Reality has a way of proving us wrong in this area. We actually think God will not require some form of payment for our bad habits. This currently popular theology merely makes God into our own image—"My God would never do that to anyone." Our version of God has taken the place of who God really is.

A biblical example of such idolatry is Peter's response to Jesus upon hearing that Jesus would have to die as part of God's plan for the new Kingdom (Mark 8). Peter had other notions of how God, and, thus, Jesus, should act, in essence proclaiming, "This can't happen to me; you can't die now!" Jesus quickly reminded him that things were going to happen according to God's plan, not Peter's. This was no doubt a very difficult lesson to learn for the loyal disciple.

Second, the misperception that "I have been a good person all of my life" permeates our contemporary theology and worldview. The implication is that, because I have been good, only good will happen to me. In other words, God owes me. Both caregivers and sufferers need to ask, Does God really owe us anything? Does God always act like we want God to act?

Throughout the Bible we read of instances where both (mis)understandings are manifest. The Israelites again and again thought that, if they obeyed God's commands, they would be free from punishment. This, of course, was not the case. Recall that God sent the Assyrians to destroy Israel to punish the Israelites for their "sins." Likewise, the Israelites, as well as the early Christians, thought that, because they were God's chosen people, they were exempt from punishment. The Israelites flaunted their picture of God right in front of the deity's face!

Thus, we can see that the sin of idolatry is often in the background of God-talk.[4] The sufferer has pictured God in human terms. The God-talk, particularly in the genre of tragedy, is a way of working out and even confessing the true nature of God. Such reasoning leads to catharsis, or, spiritually speaking, conversion. False expectations and limits incorrectly placed upon God are found to be unrealistic, and this is the goal of tragedy: to get the audience to rethink their current beliefs in the light of present day realities.

God-talk, in the genre of tragedy, does the same thing. By articulating the many parameters of the tragedy, sufferers are rethinking their theology in order to make better sense of the all-too-real reality.

GOD-TALK AND THE GENRE OF PRAYER

Sometimes God-talk comes in the form of short outbursts such as "Oh, God, where are you?" and "Help me, Jesus!" While these and other similar outbursts are very familiar to caregivers, we may see such pleas as mindless babbling or irrational behavior, or even as desperate attempts to raise God's attention or to demand justice. What happens, however, when we consider them as *prayers?* In order to answer this, we must first fully understand what prayer really is.

To begin with, prayer is part of religious language. Religious language, according to Peter Donovan, is the interpretive means by which we connect the two poles of religious phenomena and religious behavior.[5] Such language is human-centered and depends upon the religious traditions (lessons, stories, scriptures) of the interpreter for its imagery. The imagery used is metaphorical and often ambiguous. The question must be asked, then, given the potential ambiguity of the metaphors, is this language truthful? Can this language be relied upon to portray an accurate picture of God?

Donovan notes that there are many ways to relate truth. Diagnosis, expression of feelings, offering advice, using analogies, employing illustrations, giving opinions, and offering interpretations are all valid ways of dispensing "truth." The search for truth in religious language, however, should not become our priority, because religious language serves a functional as well as a factual purpose. This function of religious language includes "enlightenment, release from sin, healing of mind and body, divine guidance, etc."[6]

When we focus more exclusively on prayer, we find that the description of religious language is the same as the description for prayer. According to the *Dictionary of Pastoral Care and Counseling,* prayer provides healing, meaning where meaning has been lost or confused, and a focus on the deity. It can also energize one's faith. Recalling that God initiates prayer within us even when we can't seem to pray, prayer is "what we do so that God can do something to us and with us. . . . Prayer is human language and it is fundamentally metaphorical."[7]

With this information, we have a better understanding of what prayer is, but can short outbursts uttered in the anxiety of crisis be called prayers? They do stem from human experience, they use human terms, they are directed toward God, and they do indeed cry out for something to be done. Thus, it would appear that these short statements are prayers. Specifically, I suggest that these are prayers of lament.

We can better understand these prayerful laments if we examine similar laments that occur throughout the Bible. Since biblical prayers are often uttered in the throes of crisis, an investigation of biblical prayer will help us to better understand and appreciate the prayer of lament and, consequently, the similar reactions of our clients/parishioners to the crises around them.

Samuel E. Ballentine's *Prayer in the Hebrew Bible* is most illuminating for learning about lament-style prayer.[8] Most treatments of prayer in the Bible consider only the psalms, but Ballentine examines prose-style prayers in the Old Testament in their literary context.

Ballentine's exploration of prose-style prayers initially reveals two types of prayer: liturgical, formal prayers that occur in cultic settings; and prayers that arise in times of crisis and are more informal. Compare this distinction to the calm prayers we hear and read in worship services and the everyday outbursts we hear as caregivers. This distinction is also important in that we often approach our sufferers with our formal, liturgical theology in our caregiving. When their desperate, informal, and quite irrational God-talk irrupts from the depths of their burning souls, it often contrasts directly with our more rational, learned, yet often dispassionate, theology.

Such informal prose-style prayers in the Hebrew Bible, Ballentine argues, serve as literary devices for portraying both God and the pray-er and this raises several questions for the reader of the Bible. What does the prayer say about the pray-er? How is God to be seen in this particular crisis? Why is it important to characterize God and pray-er this way? What does the writer intend to portray to the reader with this prayer? These and other questions, important for the exegete, should also be important for the caregiver in the pastoral setting when similar prayers are encountered. Why is the sufferer praying this way? What picture of God and what underlying assumptions about God are portrayed here? What does this picture of God *mean* for this individual in this particular setting?

Rather than searching through the context of that particular crisis, however, we as caregivers may intrude our own pictures of how God ought to be into the dialogue and divert our parishioner from his or her intentions and spiritual needs. One way we divert our parishioner's spiritual attention during the crisis is to suggest or even dictate that God simply does not act the way this prayer suggests God acts. In other words, we label the prayer or its content as abnormal and then offer a "normal" alternative. Past scholarly research supports this pastoral interpretation since it has likewise suggested that lament-oriented prayer in the Old Testament was a product of the perilous Babylonian exile. This observation implies that lament-style prayer is merely a product of extreme crisis and can be dismissed as out of bounds when heard in other times, such as tranquil political and social climates, and in other contexts, such as the temple worship.

Ballentine counters this misconception and suggests that lament-style prayer was most likely quite common throughout the life of Israel.[9] If it was indeed quite common, then it was not an aberration from the norm but was instead a part of the norm. Likewise, for caregivers to suggest that lament-style prayers are abnormal in that they only surface during the confusion of crisis is to neglect the fact that crisis is a very important and normal part of the whole of life.

In many instances, Ballentine shows, lament-style prayers are more conversational than formal, and it is this aspect of the prayers that seems to throw off interpreters, both biblical and pastoral, from the significance of the lament. In Biblical lament-style prayers, someone may simply call on the name of God or the passage will simply read "someone prayed, saying . . . ." Thus, what might appear to us without the literary introductions as prose, dialogue, or even frantic ejaculations is really prayer. In other biblical passages, a person simply says something to God, and this utterance, once analyzed, is observed to be a prayer.[10]

The relevance of Ballentine's conclusions for caregivers is obvious. Without the formal setting and the other signals of prayer (bowed heads, formal introductions, typical language, worship book), we may entirely miss the fact that someone is praying. Thus, what we may label as irrational gibberish in the confusion of the crisis may indeed be a prayer.

These conversational-style prayers, Ballentine argues, center around two important foci: the innocent suffering of the prayer and the demand for proof of the presence of God. Caregivers no doubt will agree that similar prayers encountered in their ministry contain these elements. These biblical prayers also readily borrow metaphors from human experience and this echoes what we have already examined in our discussion of religious language and prayer. God is depicted in these prayers in human ways, and God quite often does not act like God is "supposed" to act. Indeed, Ballentine demonstrates that God in the lament-style prayers does whatever God wants to. Such a God does not conform to our sterile, theologically reasoned images of God at all![11]

Ballentine warns against taking these human images of God too literally, lest the pastoral equivalent of exegetical stuckness occur. At the same time, he also reminds scholars and the church that we must take seriously the depiction of God in the lament-style prayer. Unfortunately, we may try to bypass or just ignore laments and their loaded God-talk altogether by standing within the relatively safe confines of "acceptable" theology. "God does not act that way," we may respond, or we may just nod our heads in fake agreement while shaking our heads in theological dissent.[12]

When such lament-style prayers are encountered in our ministry we are meeting head-on a heretofore-unseen aspect of the real person. Gone are the formal thoughts about God. The requirements of "proper" theology and worship etiquette are no longer valid. Instead, a less formal, more intimate, conversational encounter with God is taking place. This time of discernment is valuable for the caregiver and the sufferer. Both can use this time to explore the images of God that arise with this crisis. This, then, is the reason for lament-style prayers and the God talk within them. A new dialogue concerning unexpected and even undeserved aspects of life is opened with God. This is a conversation that is perhaps better left for the two individuals to complete. Our task as caregivers is at the least, to watch, and, at the most, to serve as impartial referees. Anything else rudely interrupts the conversation between sufferer and God.

GOD-TALK AND THE GENRE OF STORY

If we continue this literary interpretation of God-talk further, we must acknowledge the fact that prayer and tragedy as well as myth and apocalyptic all make extensive use of metaphor and the imagination. We have discussed the potential confusion concerning the use of metaphor and the problems with imagination in previous chapters. We have seen throughout this discussion, however, that God-talk as religious language arises during times of crisis to explain what fact or reality apparently cannot comprehend. We should now realize that the fiction of tragedy, imaginatively described through the device of metaphor, does indeed contain truth that may be trying to make better sense of the facts of life.

Conclusion: Genres of Faith

During the times of crisis our imagination comes to bat for our injured faith. Edward Robinson takes great pains to inform us that imagination and faith are actually one entity. To fully comprehend the mystery known as God, we must employ our imaginations. "The creative imagination . . . is thus our natural, inborn faculty for transcendence, for rising above the limits of what previously seemed impossible." We have already seen how tradition is important for religious language. Robinson writes that imagination and tradition are "intimately dependent upon each other." Tradition informs the imagination, keeping it within certain bounds, but also allowing it to search for new ways of expression. God-talk, well-informed by tradition, imaginatively expresses what the sufferer is feeling.[13]

Ann and Barry Ulanov take the discussion of the importance of imagination to our spiritual lives into even deeper waters of understanding. To make use of the imagination frightens many because it may lead to control or even distortion of our lives. Still, the imagination fills the gap between reality and what we hope reality will be. It takes us far away from what a restrictive religion defines as OK. "Things are constantly reborn in the imagination, made fresh, brought to us to renew themselves and to renew us." The imagination allows us to tread the perilous passage of the "Deep," the darkness, those horrifying places hidden in our souls where indeed God may be very vicious, mean, diabolical, or even passionate and loving. The imagination dwells on paradox, on oblique and contradictory things, and allows us to learn to live with them instead of denying, escaping, or destroying them. By setting the imagination free, we turn loose our spiritual inhibitions and let be what really is. Imagination, the Ulanovs write, "makes us ask how the old official pictures of God touch, inform, confront our personal god-images, and how our own images touch, confront, inform those of tradition."[14]

With this in mind, consider these creative interpretations of tragedy:

- I guess God had a need for Billy, so he took him away from us.
- Those trees fell all about the house, but God must have been in that storm because our house was not even scratched.
- This life is so short, but there she can praise God for an eternity.

We have no doubt heard many such creative, imaginative thoughts about how and why God did certain things to people. If we consider these sayings as story we can better comprehend their purpose. Author Madeleine L'Engle writes that the basis of all story is "What if?" Throughout this book we have noted how sufferers, when trying to make sense of their tragedies and their previous theologies, ask new questions such as, "What if God takes people when God wants to?" With this beginning question we are then encouraged to "write" a story that fills in the rest of the blank in our shattered life. Our imaginations take over our previously rational aids and begin a search for new answers.[15]

L'Engle goes on to compare the conscious mind to the iceberg. What our conscious—our fact-oriented mind—perceives is really quite small compared to the vast, dark regions of the subconscious mind underneath the waters of cultural or social conformity. Her dependence upon Jung here is quite obvious. By writing a story, by delving into "fiction," we utilize the many images that are available in our subconscious mind. With this process, we can arrive at a better understanding of our tragedy. We have already noted in a previous chapter how artists, and thus writers, writing out of deep personal pain and tragedy, can often perceive and give voice to what many fail to comprehend. If we treat the God-talkers before us as creative writers, we can begin to better understand what they are saying and why they must say it.

L'Engle, echoing what we have already learned, declares that theologians are perhaps the worst for insisting that God acts in only one way. Those who have been through tragedy, who originally believed that God was rational, ordered, and full of justice, have now been exposed to a different side of God. What does this do now for their picture of God? "What if . . . ?" they ask as they begin to write a new story that seeks to arrive at a better understanding of the world, an understanding that more precisely explains what has happened to them. The "What if . . . ?" is, I would argue, the positive use of God-talk to rewrite our theology in order to fit the present actions of God.

Eugene H. Peterson puts this same argument into a biblical perspective. Most of our theology, he observes, comes from the "big" stories in the Bible. Creation, exodus, settlement, prophecies, the life, death, and resurrection of Christ, the struggles of the early Christians—these are the major influences in our spiritual lives. Nearly all of our theology is centered around these stories. Unfortunately, sometimes people do not fit into these stories. Does the church ignore them, either leaving them out of the church's story or by insisting that they conform to the church's theology? What if the church's theology/story does not provide pastoral comfort to them? Are they or the church to blame?[16]

These are important questions and their relevance is nowhere more manifest than in the area of pastoral care. Peterson notes that the story of Ruth does not fit into the major categories of faith found in the Bible. There is no major crisis (biblically speaking, anyway), "no outstanding, historically prominent figures in Ruth, no splendid kings, no charismatic judges, no fiery prophets." Not to mention the fact that Ruth is a *short story*. Its very genre makes it unique in the scriptures.[17]

Yet, the short story of Ruth is in the Bible, and thus it shows that everyday, ordinary life is also part of God's ultimate concern. For people who do not think they fit within the major foci of the church, and this would certainly include sufferers reduced to the nontraditional language of God-talk to express the tragedy in their lives, the short story, "by beginning where they are and concentrating on the problem of their life-situation . . . is able to shape the details of their particular suffering or despair or emptiness into a connected, ordered story that can be, then, seen as an aspect of the larger narration." When the story is narrated to us, we should not stoop to moralisms or condescensions. Instead we should merely affirm the story and "provide the opportunity and stimulus for persons to construct and tell their own stories as personal and locate instances of the story of covenant salvation."[18]

These, then, are just a few genres of faith. If we look at God-talk as a person's attempt to write a new theology of God, then we can better understand why such genres are used by believers during times of crisis. Their current theology, though quite rational and even correct by society's ordinarily acceptable standards, does not adequately interpret what has happened to them. Thus, they turn to the unordinary language of the people—mythical thoughts of God that are indeed tragic, informal, conversational prayers, apocalyptic and prosaic, that are not reasoned dissertations, theological treatises or formal thoughts but are instead simply talk—conversation, stories. By using these various genres of faith, the sufferer can explain, and thus achieve some sense of control over, the present crisis.

As the sufferer relates a personal tragedy, we can explore how this tragic story has changed the sufferer's perceptions of God. How will this image and its implied theology affect the spiritual life of the sufferer? As with some dreams, the conclusions may be off base, but most likely the person will have a new and more realistic perception about life and God. When confronted with the short laments of God-talk we should allow these words to rise freely to God. Encourage the sufferer to ask questions regarding such statements. What are you saying about God? Are you ready to accept such an image of God? The answers may help us discern what direction the sufferer needs to take for spiritual healing to occur. If there are still some theological hesitations about the crisis, then we can help our parishioners to "write out" the story of their tragedy. What if God really does want your child? What if God has a purpose for taking this away from you?

By viewing God-talk as literary faith genres, we can encourage an open-ended, imaginative healing story process in the aftermath of tragedy. This theological journey will allow the sufferer to edit the pages of his or her life story as it is written by the very Author of Life.

Notes

Introduction

1. Donald Capps, *Reframing: A New Method in Pastoral Care* (Minneapolis: Fortress Press, 1990). I am summarizing Chapter 1 in this discussion. Quotes in the following discussion are from pp. 14, 18.

2. Philosopher Peter Kreeft, *Making Sense Out of Suffering* (Ann Arbor, MI: Servant Books, 1986), p. 55, for example, also notes that we need to change the question from "Why?" but he argues that we need instead to ask "Whom?" as in "Who is in charge of this tragedy?"

3. James M. Efird, *These Things Are Written: An Introduction to the Religious Ideas of the Bible* (Atlanta: John Knox Press, 1978), p. 19, warns about confusing the New Testament idea of agape love with the Old Testament idea of *hesed* love. "Too often, however, this love has been sentimentalized either into a slushy concept of self-depreciation, or, an idealized view that love conquers all!" See also Kreeft, *Making Sense,* especially Chapter 4 and his section on Boethius and Chapter 6 in which he arrives at the same conclusions, through philosophical arguments and other sources, that Capps makes from a therapeutic perspective. For a thorough psychological discussion of how our society came to confuse the biblical idea of love with the idolatrous humanistic love see Paul C. Vitz, *Psychology As Religion: The Cult of Self-Worship* (Grand Rapids, MI: William B. Eerdmans Publishing Co., 1977, 1994), Chapter 8 and p. 132ff.

4. See "Terror Times Two," Michael Elliott, August 17, 1998, *Newsweek,* pp. 22-28.

5. Wayne E. Oates, *Luck: A Secular Faith* (Louisville, KY: Westminster John Knox Press, 1995).

6. *United Church News,* National Edition, Vol. XV, No. 4, pp. 1 and 9.

7. Howard W. Stone, *Theological Context for Pastoral Caregiving* (Binghamton, NY: The Haworth Pastoral Press, 1996), Chapter 8. Stone admits that he, too, has backed away from the "Why?" questions in his pastoral ministry. ". . . I discovered that I had a repertoire of fairly safe ways for ignoring them or changing the subject," p. 127.

8. Frederick Sontag, "Anthropodicy and the Return of God," in Stephen T. Davis (Ed.), *Encountering Evil: Live Options in Theodicy* (Atlanta: John Knox Press, 1981), pp. 137-166, quotes from pp. 139, 140, 148, respectively.

9. Charles V. Gerkin, *The Living Human Document: Re-Visioning Pastoral Counseling in a Hermeneutical Mode* (Nashville, TN: Abingdon Press, 1984).

10. Walter Brueggemann, *Theology of the Old Testament: Testimony, Dispute, Advocacy* (Minneapolis: Fortress Press, 1997), pp. 82-84.

11. The term "the Satan" is the generally accepted use of this phrase as represented in the book of Job. The idea is that "the Satan" is a technical term, such as "the plumber" or "the beautician." The role of a satan is to be an adversary, one who accuses a person, as in the role of a prosecuting attorney (Zechariah 3:1ff.). By the time of the New Testament, "the Satan" had achieved a greater status as the cosmic adversary of God.

12. One example of how the other side of tragedy brought about a concurrent change in theology and interpretation of the divine personality can be found in the exilic prophets. Ezekiel, preaching and providing pastoral care to the exiles, taught that the corporate Israel would no longer be held accountable for sin but instead the individual would be held accountable (Ezekiel 18:4ff.). This comes in direct contrast to the former theology which stated the sins of the fathers would be handed down to the third and fourth generation (Exodus 20:5). Such a new way of thinking echoes Capps' second order change because the system itself has changed (*Reframing*, p. 12).

13. See the table of faith development in James Fowler, *Stages of Faith: The Psychology of Human Development and the Quest for Meaning* (San Francisco: Harper & Row, 1981), p. 52. Interestingly, Fowler labels the highest level of human spiritual development "Wisdom."

14. Much of this work is based on the growing, postmodern assessment of the Enlightenment and its effects on our society and culture. In short, the rational, positivistic, scientific thought of the modern era has not lived up to the expectations of the Enlightenment and has sapped our spiritual lives of mystery and faith. I will only list a few examples of such critiques. For an assessment of how Enlightenment thought has skewed biblical interpretation, see Brueggemann, *Theology,* Chapter 2; for a psychological critique of humanistic thought, see Vitz, *Psychology,* Chapters 8-10; Theologian Jurgen Moltmann, *Theology of Hope: On the Ground and Implications of a Christian Theology* (Minneapolis: Fortress Press, 1993), especially Chapter 1, notes that Enlightenment thinkers removed the element of hope, as found in apocalyptic and eschatological themes in the Bible, from theology; a philosophical critique of Enlightenment thought in regard to suffering may be found in Kreeft, *Making Sense;* for a general critique of liberal arts education and how it has affected our culture, see Allan Bloom, *The Closing of the American Mind: How Higher Education Has Failed Democracy and Impoverished the Souls of Today's Students* (New York: Simon and Schuster, 1987).

Chapter 1

1. Robert McAfee Brown, "Dear Mackenzie: A Message to My Granddaughter," *Christian Century* 11(7), March 2, 1994, pp. 227-228. See the response by Langford Baldwin, "An Impotent God?" in *Christian Century* 11(19), June 15-22, 1994, pp. 620-622 which includes a response by Brown. The dialogue focuses on the issues of God-talk as elaborated in this chapter.

2. Harold Kushner, *When Bad Things Happen to Good People* (New York: Avon Books, 1981).

3. Interestingly, Simon J. deVries, "Evil," in *Interpreter's Dictionary of the Bible* Vol. 2, pp. 182-183, notes that evil as related in the Bible has a pragmatic purpose. See also O. A. Piper, "Suffering and Evil," *IDB* Vol. 4, pp. 450-453, who explains that, throughout the Bible, suffering and evil are seen either as the results of sin or as acts of God. Thus, there is a divine purpose in suffering and evil if the faithful believer is willing to search for it. Piper also explains that modern distinctions between natural and moral evil are foreign to the Bible. For an example of how modern sensibilities often dictate our responses to the divinely caused problems of suffering and evil see James L. Crenshaw, "Introduction: The Shift from Theodicy to Anthropodicy," in Crenshaw, (Ed.), *Theodicy in the Old Testament*, Issues in Religion and Theology 4 (Philadelphia: Fortress Press, 1983), pp. 1-16. Here Crenshaw raises questions concerning the defense of God and how such defenses bring with them the loss of human integrity. He is willing to sacrifice the sovereignty of God in order to retain the integrity of humans. For a contrary opinion, see Frederick Sontag, "Anthropodicy and the Return of God," in Stephen T. Davis (Ed.), *Encountering Evil: Live Options in Theodicy* (Atlanta: John Knox Press, 1981), pp. 137-166. Crenshaw represents the type of pastoral response that misses the integrity and meaning of God-talk while Sontag argues that we have for too long allowed the sovereignty of God to take second place to the integrity of humanity.

4. Brown, "Dear Mackenzie," p. 227.

5. Peter Kreeft, *Making Sense Out of Suffering* (Ann Arbor, MI: Servant Books, 1986), Chapter 10 and throughout the book. This is the most practical, realistic, and sensible book on suffering I have read.

6. Ruth Nanda Anshen, *The Reality of the Devil: Evil in Man* (New York: Harper & Row, 1972), pp. xiv-xv.

7. Sontag, "Anthropodicy," pp. 137-166.

8. Brown, "Dear Mackenzie," p. 227.

9. Ibid, p. 228.

10. This quote from St. Augustine is found in the writings of Thomas Aquinas, as mentioned in Kreeft, *Making Sense,* p. 91. Kreeft does not provide bibliographical information for this quote.

11. It will be seen throughout this work that choice is a key ingredient in recovering from suffering in the grief process. For an example of choosing to see God's hand in tragedy, see Wendy Murray Zoba's article on the Columbine tragedy "Do You Believe in God?" in *Christianity Today,* 43(11) (October 11, 1999), pp. 32-43. In following with Capps' insistence on ignoring questions of "why?" and instead seeking to pursue the "what?" of posttragic suffering, note the reaction of one of the pastors of the surviving families who states, "The hardest thing for me sitting with this family—they are very nice people—is to turn off the switch in my head and not pursue the *why?* and just listen . . ." (p. 39). This is a clear example of choice and how it leads to second order change in pastoral care.

12. Brown, "Dear Mackenzie," pp. 227-228.

13. See, for example, David F. Wells, *Losing Our Virtue: Why the Church Must Recover Its Moral Vision* (Grand Rapids, MI: William B. Eerdmans Publishing Co., 1998), Chapter 2, especially p. 43.

14. To be fair to the *Christian Century*, not all of its reporting takes this rational line that I am critiquing. In the past several years there has been a slow shift toward the middle of this theological spectrum. For example, see the report from Kenya on the bombing in Nairobi where God and Jesus are praised for their help in the crisis (*Christian Century*, 115(24) [September 9-16, 1998]). The addition of Miroslav Volf's reflections have also rendered a more open view of God's involvement in life's tragedies.

15. Madeleine L'Engle, *The Rock That Is Higher: Story As Truth*, Wheaton Literary Series (Wheaton, IL: Harold Shaw Publishers, 1993).

16. Ibid., pp. 175, 11.

17. See L'Engle, *Walking on Water: Reflections on Faith and Art* (Wheaton, IL: Harold Shaw Publishers, 1980), pp. 13, 15. She goes on to note that "God is in control, no matter what, that ultimately all shall be well, no matter what," pp. 156-157.

18. For examples, see the chapter "Probable Impossibles" in *Walking* and *The Rock*, pp. 19-22, where she discusses the need for ambiguity and mystery in the Gospels. In the chapter "Story As the Search for Truth," she likewise explores the various ways story abounds in paradox and mystery, yet it reveals more truth than reason. The themes of paradox and fact versus fiction are quite abundant in her nonfiction works.

19. Kreeft, *Making Sense*, pp. 37, 48ff.; Garrett Green, *Imagining God: Theology and the Religious Imagination* (Grand Rapids, MI: William B. Eerdmans Publishing Co., 1989, 1998), pp. 92ff.; Walter Brueggemann, *Theology of the Old Testament: Testimony, Dispute, Advocacy* (Minneapolis: Fortress Press, 1997), p. 59, and Chapter 2; Gary Dorrien, *The Word As True Myth: Interpreting Modern Theology* (Louisville, KY: Westminster John Knox Press, 1997).

20. L'Engle, *The Rock*, pp. 30, 22-23, 48, 93, and 63.

21. Rudolf Otto, *The Idea of the Holy: An inquiry into the non-rational factor in the idea of the divine and its relation to the rational*, trans. John W. Harvey (London: Oxford University Press, 1923, 1958).

22. L'Engle, *The Rock*, pp. 100, 222.

23. Ibid., p. 205.

24. Ibid., p. 176.

25. Kreeft, *Making Sense*, p. 78.

26. Eugene H. Peterson, *Five Smooth Stones for Pastoral Work* (Atlanta: John Knox Press, 1980), pp. 93, 119. Peterson has many trenchant thoughts for pastoral caregivers in this chapter.

27. L'Engle, *The Rock*, p. 100.

28. The term A-rational is intentional. The point here is that God is neither rational nor irrational since both terms imply that God conforms to our ways of understanding. Thus, a more realistic term would be A-rational. For an intriguing examination of

such atypical theological terminology see Mark C. Taylor, *Erring: A Postmodern A/theology* (Chicago: University of Chicago Press, 1984.)

29. Martin E. Marty, *A Cry of Absence: Reflections for the Winter of the Heart* (Grand Rapids, MI: William B. Eerdmans Publishing Co., 1983), pp. ix, xvi.

30. As Randall J. Vander Mey laments in *God-Talk: The Triteness and Truth in Christian Cliches* (Downers Grove, IL: InterVarsity Press, 1993), pp. 182-186.

31. As Wells, *Losing Our Virtue,* p. 50, points out.

32. Marty, *Absence,* p. 6.

33. See Charles V. Gerkin, *The Living Human Document: Re-Visioning Pastoral Counseling in a Hermeneutical Mode* (Nashville, TN: Abingdon Press, 1984) for an example of this pastoral method.

34. Marty, *Absence,* Chapter 2.

35. Ibid., pp. 4-5.

36. There are ample examples of such initiation processes. For a social interpretation, see Emile Durkheim, *The Elementary Forms of the Religious Life,* trans. Joseph Ward Swain (New York: The Free Press, 1965), especially Book Three, "The Principle Ritual Attitudes"; for an analysis of the sacred and the profane and their religious implications see Mircea Eliade, *The Sacred and the Profane: The Nature of Religion,* trans. Willard R. Trask (New York: Harcourt Brace Jovanovich, 1959). Once one is touched by God, either through tragedy or initiation, the person is too holy (sacred) for the (profane) community and must be banished into a sacred time or territory where he or she endures a spiritual wilderness experience until ready to come back into the profane world of the community.

37. This phrase is intentionally mythical. For examples of such interpretations of tragedy and suffering, see Mircea Eliade, *The Myth of the Eternal Return (Cosmos and History),* trans. Willard R. Trask, Bollingen Series XLVI (Princeton: Princeton University Press, 1973), Chapter 3, "Misfortune and History"; see also Jon D. Levenson, *Creation and the Persistence of Evil: The Jewish Drama of Divine Omnipotence* (Princeton: Princeton University Press, 1988).

38. Marty, *Absence,* pp. 15, 115, 183, and especially 135.

39. Ibid., p. 39.

40. C. S. Lewis, *A Grief Observed* (New York: Bantam Books, 1976), pp. 1, 15.

41. Ibid., pp. 5, 15-16, 20, 23.

42. Ibid., p. 26.

43. Ibid., pp. 28-29.

44. Ibid., p. 35.

45. Jane Mary Zwerner, "The Discovery of Christian Meaning in Suffering: Transformation and Solidarity," in William Cenkner (Ed.), *Evil and the Response of World Religion* (St. Paul, MN: Paragon House, 1997), p. 50.

46. Quote from David J. Goldberg, "Providence and the Problem of Evil in Jewish Thought," in Cenkner, *Evil,* p. 42.

47. Lewis, *Grief,* pp. 42, 50, 53.

48. Ibid., p. 57.

49. Harold S. Kushner, *When Bad Things Happen to Good People* (New York: Avon Books, 1981).
50. Ibid., p. 2.
51. Ibid., p. 3.
52. Ibid., pp. 4, 19, 24, and Chapter 3.
53. These suggestions are not made haphazardly. The world's religions, including Judaism and Christianity, suggest such necessity for evil and suffering. See, for example, Cenkner (Ed.), *Evil and the Response of World Religion,* passim.
54. See Kreeft, *Making Sense,* for an assessment of both Kushner and our approach to theodicy, the justice of God, from this angle.
55. Kushner, *When Bad Things,* p. 4.
56. Ibid., p. 10.
57. Ibid., pp. 22ff., 81.
58. Ibid., Chapter 4.
59. Ibid., p. 29.
60. Ibid., p. 57.
61. Ibid., p. 82.
62. Ibid., p. 134.
63. I am not alone in my critical assessment of Rabbi Kushner's work. See, for example, Jeffrey R. Zurheide, *When Faith Is Tested,* Creative Pastoral Care and Counseling Series (Minneapolis: Fortress Press, 1997), pp. 30-34; Douglas John Hall, *God and Human Suffering: An Exercise in the Theology of the Cross* (Minneapolis: Augsburg Publishing House, 1986), pp. 150ff. Both authors point out that the major flaw in Kushner's work is his denial of the omnipotence of God and the consequences of faith and hope at the time of suffering.
64. Elie Weisel and Phillipe de Saint-Cheron, *Evil and Exile,* trans. Jon Rothschild (Notre Dame, IN: University of Notre Dame Press, 1990), pp. 1-33.

Chapter 2

1. Daniel Liderbach, *Why Do We Suffer? New Ways of Understanding* (New York: Paulist Press, 1992).
2. John Macquarrie, *God-Talk: An Examination of the Language and Logic of Theology* (New York: Harper & Row, 1967), p. 11.
3. Howard W. Stone, *Theological Context for Pastoral Caregiving: Word in Deed* (Binghamton, NY: The Haworth Pastoral Press, 1996), Chapter 8, notes that caregivers often resort to comfortable theologies when confronted with suffering and thus the total context of the pastoral encounter should help caregivers decide how to proceed and what to say.
4. Macquarrie, *God-Talk,* pp. 65-66, 120ff. See James Barr, *The Semantics of Biblical Language* (Oxford: Oxford University Press, 1961).
5. Macquarrie, *God-Talk,* p. 66.

6. Ibid., p. 70 and Chapter 6. For a similar approach from a pastoral theologian, see Charles V. Gerkin, *Prophetic Pastoral Practice: A Christian Vision of Life Together* (Nashville, TN: Abingdon Press, 1991), Chapters 1-3.

7. Macquarrie, *God-Talk,* p. 75.

8. Ibid, p. 80

9. Ibid., pp. 80, 89.

10. Ibid., p. 18.

11. Liderbach, *Why? passim.*

12. Macquarrie, *God-Talk,* p. 14.

13. For a technical discussion of God-images, see M. Katherine Armistead, *God-Images in the Healing Process* (Minneapolis, MN: Fortress Press, 1995).

14. It is well known in texts on the wisdom literature of the Bible that the story of Joseph contains elements of wisdom. Thus many scholars place the story within the genre of Wisdom Literature. See, for example, the discussions by Gerhard von Rad, *Wisdom in Israel* (Nashville, TN: Abingdon, 1972), pp. 44ff. and James L. Crenshaw, *Old Testament Wisdom: An Introduction,* rev. and enl. (Louisville, KY: Westminster John Knox Press, 1998), p. 29. For an investigation of the contemplative side of the Wisdom Literature, see John Eaton, *The Contemplative Face of Old Testament Wisdom: In the Context of World Religions* (London: SCM Press, 1989), especially Chapter 2.

15. Wayne E. Oates, *Luck,* pp. 8-10, 35-37, and throughout the book. Stone, *Theological Context,* pp. 141ff. Note that Stone suggests that questions of Why? are often poetic, thus they do not warrant an answer so much as they simply give vent to a deep emotional pain. Reflection upon God-talk will reveal that much of what we are asked in a crisis is really rhetorical and that, since we are being asked in metaphorical language, we should respond likewise.

16. Macquarrie, *God-Talk,* pp. 22, 27.

17. Liderbach, *Why?,* Chapter 5; Macquarrie, *God-Talk,* p. 30.

18. Macquarrie, *God-Talk,* pp. 169, 180-181. For an example of how modern myths parallel religious myths see George Johnson, *Fire in the Mind: Science, Faith, and the Search for Order* (New York: Alfred A. Knopf, 1995).

19. Liderbach, *Why?,* p. 98.

20. Gary Dorrien, *The Word As True Myth: Interpreting Modern Theology* (Louisville, KY: Westminster John Knox Press, 1997).

21. Ibid., p. 15.

22. Liderbach, *Why?,* pp. 75, 83, 89; Oscar Cullmann, *Prayer in the New Testament,* Overtures to Biblical Theology (Minneapolis, MN: Fortress Press, 1995), pp. 72ff.

23. Dorrien, *True Myth,* p. 71.

24. Huston Smith, *Forgotten Truth: The Common Vision of the World's Religions* (San Francisco: Harper, 1976, 1992), "Taken in its entirety, the world is not as science says it is; it is as science, philosophy, religion, the arts, and everyday speech say it is," p. 16; Dorrien, *True Myth,* p. 198.

25. Dorrien, *True Myth,* pp. 88, 94, 117.

26. Ibid., pp. 121, 140.
27. Liderbach, *Why?*, p. 13 and throughout; Gerkin, *Prophetic*, Chapters 1-3.
28. Dorrien, pp. 160, 177. For an exploration of psychology as a religion, see Paul C. Vitz, *Psychology As Religion: The Cult of Self-Worship*, Second Edition (Grand Rapids, MI: William B. Eerdmans Publishing Co., 1997, 1994).
29. Dorrien, *True Myth*, p. 225.
30. Ibid., p. 226.
31. For the mythical, theological explanation of this interpretation of Jesus Christ, see Paul Tillich, *Systematic Theology*, Vol. II, "Existence and the Christ" (Chicago: The University of Chicago Press, 1957).
32. Garrett Green, *Imagining God: Theology and the Religious Imagination*, Chapter 7 (Grand Rapids, MI: William B. Eerdmans Publishing Co., 1989, 1998).
33. Ibid., p. 123.
34. Ibid., pp. 133-134.
35. Ibid., p. 139.
36. Ibid., p. 140.
37. Ibid., p. 144.
38. Ibid., p. 151.

Chapter 3

1. For example, J. Bill Ratliff, *When You Are Facing Change* (Louisville, KY: John Knox Press, 1989), p. 49: "I do not believe that God causes sufferings or brings traumatic transitions upon us."
2. James L. Crenshaw, *A Whirlpool of Torment: Israelite Traditions of God As an Oppressive Presence*, Overtures to Biblical Theology 12 (Philadelphia: Fortress Press, 1984); W. Lee Humphreys, *The Tragic Vision and the Hebrew Tradition*, Overtures to Biblical Theology 18 (Philadelphia: Fortress Press, 1985).
3. D. W. Foy, "Survivor Psychology," in Rodney J. Hunter (Gen. Ed.), *Dictionary of Pastoral Care and Counseling* (Nashville, TN: Abingdon Press, 1990), pp. 1245-1247.
4. David K. Switzer, *The Minister As Crisis Counselor* (Nashville, TN: Abingdon Press, 1974), pp. 41-43.
5. Mark S. Smith, *The Early History of God: Yahweh and the Other Deities in Ancient Israel* (San Francisco: Harper & Row, 1990). I employ his conclusions throughout this discussion. See also Frank Moore Cross, *Canaanite Myth and Hebrew Epic: Essays in the History of the Religion of Israel* (Cambridge, MA: Harvard University Press, 1973).
6. Humphreys, *Vision*, p. xiv, also notes that the tragic vision from Israel's traditions likewise arose during times of political/social duress, especially during and after the exile.
7. Jon D. Levenson, *Creation and the Persistence of Evil: The Jewish Drama of Divine Omnipotence* (Princeton: Princeton University Press, 1988).

8. Jack Sasson, *Anchor Bible,* Vol. 24B, "Jonah," (New York: Doubleday, 1990), pp. 90ff.

9. See, for example, G. B. Caird, *Harper's New Testament Commentaries,* "A Commentary on the Revelation of St. John the Divine" (New York: Harper & Row, 1966). Caird struggles passionately to make sense of the tension between the power of God and the rampant destruction of the creation as revealed by God to John.

10. Recall Martin E. Marty's series of reflection on the absence of God in *A Cry of Absence: Reflections on the Winter of the Heart* (Grand Rapids, MI: William B. Eerdmans Publishing Co., 1983, 1987).

11. For instance, Artur Weiser, *The Old Testament Library,* "The Psalms," (Philadelphia: Westminster Press, 1971), p. 271.

12. See J. Christian Beker, *Suffering and Hope: The Biblical Vision and the Human Predicament* (Grand Rapids, MI: William B. Eerdmans Publishing Co., 1994) for a breakdown of this particular theology and various other theologies of suffering in the Bible.

13. For a similar interpretation of Job, see Gustavo Gutierrez, *On Job: God-Talk and the Suffering of the Innocent* (Maryknoll, NY: Orbis Books, 1987).

14. I have mentioned the drawbacks of Enlightenment thought throughout this work. Beker, *Suffering,* in his discussion of Paul and suffering, notes the accusations of idolatry by the apostle. For a psychological explanation of this phenomenon, see Paul C. Vitz, *Psychology As Religion: The Cult of Self-Worship,* Second Edition (Grand Rapids, MI: William B. Eerdmans Publishing Co., 1994), who discusses how Enlightenment thought has led to the current fad of self-worship; thus, we idolize ourselves.

Chapter 4

1. Morton Kelsey, *Discernment: A Study in Ecstasy and Evil* (New York: Paulist Press, 1978).

2. Ibid., pp. 98-100.

3. Ibid. I will be discussing at length Chapter 4, "Language, Myth, and Evil," pp. 86-105.

4. Rudolf Otto, *The Idea of the Holy,* trans. John W. Harvey (London: Oxford University Press, 1923, 1958), pp. 1-45, 77-80.

5. I have summarized the thoughts of several scholars here. On the "dumbing down" of God, see Donald McCullough, *The Trivialization of God: The Dangerous Illusion of a Manageable Deity* (Colorado Springs, CO: NAVPRESS, 1995); for a theological critique of our society's spiritual trend and its lack of theological depth, see David F. Wells, *Losing Our Virtue: Why the Church Must Recover Its Moral Vision* (Grand Rapids, MI: William B. Eerdmans Publishing Company, 1998); for a psychological critique of the pop-psychology movement, see Paul C. Vitz, *Psychology As Religion: The Cult of Self-Worship,* Second Edition (Grand Rapids, MI: William B. Eerdmans Publishing Co., 1977, 1994); for an investigation into the removal of the attribute of vengeance from the character of God, see Erich Zenger,

A God of Vengeance? Understanding the Psalms of Divine Wrath (Louisville, KY: Westminster John Knox Press, 1996).

6. Carl E. Braaten, (Ed.), *Our Naming of God: Problems and Prospects of God-Talk Today* (Philadelphia: Fortress Press, 1989), p. 11.

7. Kelsey, *Discernment*, pp. 91-92.

8. See Gisela Labouvie-Vief, "Wisdom as integrated thought: Historical and developmental perspectives," in Robert J. Sternberg, (Ed.), *Wisdom: Its Nature, Origins, and Development* (New York: Cambridge University Press, 1990), pp. 52-83.

9. Daniel N. Robinson, "Wisdom through the ages," in Sternberg, *Wisdom*, p. 20.

10. Mihaly Csikszenthmihalyi and Kevin Rathunde, "The psychology of wisdom: evolutionary interpretation" in Sternberg, *Wisdom*, pp. 25-51, quote from p. 35.

11. Karen Strohm Kitchener and Helene G. Brenner, "Wisdom and Reflective Judgment: knowing in the face of uncertainty," in Sternberg, (Ed.), *Wisdom*, pp. 212-229.

12. Kelsey, *Discernment*, pp. 92, 94.

13. Ibid., p. 95.

14. For an excellent explanation of how religious myths employ the same methodology as scientific theories, see Huston Smith, *Forgotten Truth: The Common Vision of the World's Religions* (New York: Harper & Row, 1992), Chapter 6.

15. H. and H. A. Frankfort, *The Intellectual Adventure of Ancient Man* (Chicago: The University of Chicago Press, 1977), pp. 1-11.

16. Allan Bloom, *The Closing of the American Mind* (New York: Simon and Schuster, 1987), pp. 227-230; Martin E. Marty, *A Cry of Absence: Reflections for the Winter of the Heart* (Grand Rapids, MI: William B. Eerdmans Publishing Co., 1997), p. 60. I am obviously not against therapy, but it is becoming more and more apparent that we are using therapy to explain what simply cannot be explained rather than using therapy to help us live with the larger ambiguities of life. The incorporation of myth into the therapeutic encounter would greatly enhance our ministry.

17. Zenger, *God of Vengeance*, throughout.

18. S.J. deVries, "Evil," in *The Interpreter's Dictionary of the Bible*, Vol. 2, pp. 182-183, writes, "Evil . . . is often spoken of as a punishment or chastisement sent from God." God uses evil for wise purposes: Thus, God is seen as the author of evil. Interestingly, in Isaiah 45:7, where we read the passage that talks of God creating both weal and woe, as most translations interpret this passage, the words in Hebrew are *shalom* and *ra*. Thus, God is the maker of peace and evil.

19. Kees W. Bolle, "Myth," in Mircea Eliade, (Ed.), *Encyclopedia of Religion*, Vol. 10, pp. 261-273.

20. Mircea Eliade, *Myth and Reality* (New York: Harper & Row, 1963) Chapter VI Mythology, Ontology, History.

21. Ibid., pp. 18-19.

22. Martin Marty, *A Cry of Absence*, p. 180; Madeleine L'Engle, *The Rock That Is Higher: Story As Truth* (Wheaton, IL: Harold Shaw Publishers, 1993), p. 242; Eliade, *Myth and Reality*, pp. 13-15 and throughout the book.

23. Eliade, *Myth and Reality,* p. 32.
24. Ibid., pp. 22-23.
25. Ibid., p. 77, fn. 1.
26. Ibid., pp. 88-89.
27. Edward P. Wimberly, *Using Scripture in Pastoral Counseling* (Nashville, TN: Abingdon Press, 1994), Chapter 1, especially p. 11.
28. Eliade, *Myth,* pp. 81-82, 92, 139, 141-143.
29. Samuel Terrien, *Till the Heart Sings* (Philadelphia: Fortress Press, 1985), Chapter 5.
30. Claus Westermann, *Genesis 1-11: A Commentary,* trans. J.J. Scullion (Minneapolis: Augsburg Publishing House, 1984), p. 21.
31. Leo G. Purdue, *Wisdom and Creation: The Theology of Wisdom Literature* (Nashville, TN: Abingdon Press, 1994), p. 35.

Chapter 5

1. See D. S. Russell, *The Method and Message of Jewish Apocalyptic,* Old Testament Library (Philadelphia: The Westminster Press, 1964), pp. 19, 88ff. and Chapter 4.
2. Ibid., p. 102.
3. Tex Sample, *Hard-Living People and Mainstream Christians* (Nashville, TN: Abingdon Press, 1993), Chapter 4.
4. John J. Collins, "Apocalyptic Eschatology As the Transcendence of Death," in Paul D. Hanson (Ed.), *Visionaries and Their Apocalypses,* Issues in Religion and Theology 2 (Philadelphia: Fortress Press, 1983), pp. 61-84. Quotes from pp. 66, 68, and 78.
5. Jurgen Moltmann, *Theology of Hope: On the Ground and the Implications of a Christian Eschatology* (Minneapolis: Fortress Press, 1993), pp. 42-45, quote from p. 43.
6. Russell, *Method,* Chapter 1, quotes from pp. 16-17.
7. Helmut Koester, *Introduction to the New Testament,* Vol. 2, "History and Literature of Early Christianity" (New York: Walter De Gruyter, 1987), Chapter 12, especially p. 250.
8. Russell, *Method,* Chapter 3.
9. Jon D. Levenson, *Creation and the Persistence of Evil: The Jewish Drama of Divine Omnipotence* (Princeton: Princeton University Press, 1988), p. 32.
10. See Klaus Koch, "What Is Apocalyptic? An Attempt at a Preliminary Definition," in Hanson (Ed.), *Visionaries,* p. 23.
11. Donald Capps, *Reframing: A New Method in Pastoral Care* (Minneapolis: Fortress Press, 1990).
12. See Levenson, *Creation,* Part I, especially Chapters 3 and 4.
13. For example, Gerhard von Rad, *Wisdom in Israel* (Nashville, TN: Abingdon Press, 1972), pp. 263-283.

14. Jonathan Z. Smith, "Wisdom and Apocalyptic," in Hanson (Ed.), *Visionaries*, pp. 101-120.

15. Paul D. Hanson, "Introduction," in *Visionaries*, pp. 2-3.

16. Stephen L. Cook, *Prophecy and Apocalypticism: The Postexilic Social Setting* (Minneapolis: Fortress Press, 1995), pp. 1-4.

17. Ibid., p. 3-5. The list of Old Testament scholars who hold such positions is a virtual who's who in seminary required readings: Julius Wellhausen, Hermann Gunkel, Sigmund Mowinckel, H. H. Rowley and D. S. Russell. Thus, their influence is pervasive in ministerial studies.

18. Helmut Koester, *Introduction*, pp. 252-253.

19. For example, see Howard W. Stone, *Theological Context for Pastoral Caregiving* (Binghamton, NY: The Haworth Pastoral Press, 1996), p. 128.

20. J. J. Collins, "Apocalyptic," in Hanson (Ed.), *Visionaries*, p. 76.

21. Andrew D. Lester, *Hope in Pastoral Care and Counseling* (Louisville, KY: Westminster/John Knox Press, 1995).

22. Tom Beaudoin, *Virtual Faith: The Irreverent Spiritual Quest of Generation X* (San Francisco: Jossey-Bass, 1998). Beaudoin's interpretive technique is quite informative for the pastoral caregiver who struggles to make sense of apocalyptic images, not to mention the Generation X population.

23. Adele Yarbro Collins, *Crisis and Catharsis: The Power of the Apocalypse* (Philadelphia: Westminster Press, 1984), pp. 141-161.

24. I am aware that Ezekiel claims that the present suffering is brought about by the sufferer's actions, (i.e., sins), but the analogy is still informative for the pastoral caregiver. The greater issue in this case may be a difference of definitions. Capps, *Reframing*, p. 14, draws a distinction between a difficulty (suffering, evil, death) and a problem (a situation created because of a mishandling of a difficulty). Recall that we talk of the problem of evil as if it can be solved. But according to Capps, suffering, evil, and death are not problems that can be solved. The real issue is that a sufferer's (and also a counselor's) theology is wrong. Thus, the sufferer cannot adequately interpret the present tragedy based on these incorrect definitions. This "sin" has led to the mishandled theological interpretation of the present suffering. In a way, much of our suffering is really brought about by inadequate theologies that misinform our hearts and add unnecessary confusion to the present crisis.

Conclusion

1. W. Lee Humphreys, *The Tragic Vision and the Hebrew Tradition*, Overtures to Biblical Theology 19 (Philadelphia: Fortress Press), 1985.

2. Ibid., pp. xiv, 2.

3. Ibid., p. 7, where Humphreys notes that Aristotle's definition of tragedy includes *harmartia*, sin. Humphreys disagrees with this, however.

4. For examples of such idolatry see Donald W. McCullough, *The Trivialization of God: The Dangerous Illusion of a Manageable Deity* (Colorado Springs, CO: NAVPRESS, 1995).

5. Peter Donovan, *Religious Language* (New York: Hawthorne Books, 1976), p. 25.

6. Ibid., pp. 104, 25, 40.

7. Perry LeFevre, "Prayer," in Rodney J. Hunter (Ed.), *Dictionary of Pastoral Care and Counseling* (Nashville, TN: Abingdon Press, 1990), pp. 938-941.

8. Samuel E. Ballentine, *Prayer in the Hebrew Bible: The Drama of Divine-Human Dialogue* (Minneapolis: Fortress Press, 1993).

9. Ibid., p. 29.

10. Ibid., p. 31.

11. Ibid., pp. 19, 34, 36.

12. Ibid., p. 37.

13. Edward Robinson, *The Language of Mystery* (London: SCM Press, 1987), pp. 12, 30.

14. Ann and Barry Ulanov, *The Healing Imagination: The Meeting of Psyche and Soul* (New York: Paulist Press, 1991), p. 60.

15. Madeleine L'Engle, *Walking on Water: Reflections on Faith and Art* (Wheaton, IL: Harold Shaw Publishers, 1980), p. 105.

16. Eugene H. Peterson, *Five Smooth Stones for Pastoral Work* (Atlanta: John Knox Press, 1980), Chapter II, "The Pastoral Work of Story-making."

17. Ibid., pp. 66, 70.

18. Ibid., pp. 71-73, 76.

Index

Abraham, 4, 15
Adam and Eve, 53
Anger, 50
Angst, 60
Anshen, Ruth Nanda, 31
Anthropodicy, 16, 31, 38
Aphorisms. *See* Proverbs
Apocalyptic, 111
   as belief of the ignorant, 20
   cults, 119
   as escape, 113
   ethical, 112
   as folklore, 118
   as future hope, 113
   and Generation X, 123
   God-talk as, 17, 19
   as irrational, 121
   literature, 17
   and MTV, 123
   psychology of, 129
   as reframing, 118
   as re-mythologizing, 117
   as response of faith, 114
   vocabulary, 83
   and wisdom tradition, 118
Archetype, 53, 69, 96
   psychoreligious, 74
   as spiritual wisdom, 20
Aristotle, 133
Armistead, Katherine M., 149

Ballentine, Samuel E., 136
Barr, James, 58

Barth, Karl, 66
Beaudoin, Tom, 123
Beker, J, Christian, 151
Beliefs
   implied, 18
   religious, 17-18
   systems, 36
Bible, as authority, 69. *See also* Paradigm
Biblical passages
   New Testament
      Acts 27, 83
      1 Corinthians 10:13, 4
      2 Corinthians 11:25-26, 83
      John, 68
      Luke 8:22-25, 89
      Mark
         4: 36-41, 89
         8, 134
         8-10, 30
         13, 128
         14:32ff., 30
      Matthew 8:23-27, 89
      1 Peter, 84
         4:12-19, 127
         5:9, 31
      Revelation, 15, 83, 89, 112, 124, 128
      Romans
         9, 84
         9:14, 89
   Old Testament
      Amos, 74
      1 Chronicles 21:1, 15

Biblical passages, Old Testament
(continued)
Daniel, 127-128
Deuteronomy, 21
Ecclesiastes 6:1ff., 22
Exodus
  19, 74
  20:5, 127, 144
Ezekiel, 15, 39, 126
  18:4ff., 127, 144
Genesis
  1, 80, 89, 116
  1-3, 107, 108
  6:13, 82
  7:11, 82
  22:1-3, 4
  22:1-13, 15
  37-50, 63
  45:4ff., 132
Isaiah
  28, 74
  40-55, 39
  45:7, 14, 29, 152
  53, 107
Jeremiah 4, 74
Job, 22, 30, 62, 84, 86, 132
  38:1, 87
  38:8-11, 81, 89
  41, 116
Jonah, 15, 81
  1:4, 80
1 Kings 18, 74
1, 2 Kings, 21
Lamentations, 13, 40
Leviticus, 107
Proverbs, 21-23
Psalms, 13, 14, 29, 81
  18, 84-85
  23, 43
  42:8, 85-86
  55:8, 74
  68, 85
  74:16-17, 46
  78:2, 64
  90: 7-8 and 14, 14
  115:3, 89

Biblical passages, Old Testament,
Psalms *(continued)*
  121:1-2, 53
  130:7, 33
Ruth, 141
2 Samuel 24:1, 15
Zechariah 3:1ff., 144
Bloom, Allan, 99
Boethius, 143
Boisen, Anton, 77
Bolle, Kees W., 102
Braaten, Carl E., 94
Brenner, Helen G., 152
Brown, Robert McAfee, 28
Brueggemann, Walter, 21, 36
Bultmann, Rudolf, 66

Caird, G.B., 151
Capps, Donald, 6, 38, 117
Catharsis, 106, 126, 134
Chance, 30, 32
Change
  first and second order, 6-7
  as "uncommensensical," 7
Chaos, 3, 13, 17, 46, 54, 107
  as the Deep, 80, 82, 85
  escape of, 116
  as night, 89
  versus God, 114
Choice, 5, 33, 71, 80, 145
Christ, cross of, 30
Christian Century, 28
Cognitive dissonance, 125
Collins, Adele Yarbro, 124
Collins, John J., 113, 122
Conscious, 95, 140
Conversion, 134
Cook, Stephen L., 120
Creation, 5, 108
  design of, 29
  ex nihilo, 116
  recreation, 109
Creation stories, God-talk as, 17
Creator, 5

Crenshaw, James L., 145
Crisis
 context of, 8
 times of, 132, 139
Cross, Fran Moore, 150
Csikszenthmihalyi, Mihaly, 152
Cullman, Oscar, 65
Cults, 128. See also Apocalyptic

Daniel, 127
David, 15
de Vries, Simeon J., 145
Death, 25
 as evil, 6
 as fact of life, 6
 origin of, 103
 reason, 53
Demonic, 92
Demythology, 66
Despair, 5
Devil, 13, 17, 19, 30, 32
Difficulties, 6-7
 confusing with problems, 9
Discourse, 59. See also Language
Donovan, Peter, 135
Dorrien, Gary, 36, 64
Dualism, 112
Durkheim, Emile, 147

Eaton, John, 149
Efird, James M., 143
Eliade, Mircea, 102
Elijah, 52, 74
Enlightenment
 as idolatry, 88
 intellectualism, 31
 myths of, 34
Eschatological
 phrases, 111
 time, 20
Event
 irrational, 1
 purpose of, 9

Evil, 51, 91, 152, 154
 categories of, 92
 as a deity, 13, 17
 as fact of life, 6
 perception of, 92
 power of, 99
 problem of, 6, 13, 25, 38, 92-93
Ezekiel, 15, 62, 107, 114, 126-127

Faith. See also Genres
 bumper sticker, 41
 development, 144
 proverbial, 41
 reasoned, 5
 test of, 15
Fantasy, 18, 118-119, 122
Fate, 12, 13, 30, 32
 as nature, 47
Folk tradition, 6
Fowler, James, 144
Foy, D. W., 77

Genres, 122
 of faith, 18, 26, 131
 God-talk as, 18
 of tragedy, 132
Gerkin, Charles V., 67
Gilkey, Langdon, 67
Gnosis, 62
God, 19
 absence of, 43-44, 60
 anger of as part of God's love, 40
 angry, 2, 15
 as A-rational deity, 40
 capricious, 29, 36, 47
 as Creator, 107
 divine purpose, 37
 fairness of, 50
 fickle, 3
 of good and evil, 15, 40
 goodness, 1, 7, 51
 as idol, 94
 idol of rationality, 37

God *(continued)*
  incomprehensible, 37
  indifferent, 55
  irrational, 37, 38, 86, 93
  justice of, 31, 52
  of love, 39
  loving, 7, 29, 36
  mean, 139
  merciful, 93
  mystery, 34, 117
  play, 116
  playwright, 34
  presence of, 137
  providence of, 11, 46
  providential hands of, 9, 30
  as rationalization, 38
  as sadist, 49
  sovereignty of, 49
  as storm, 78
  triteness of, 46
  unjust, 55
  whimsical, 29, 87
  as Word, 68
  wrath of, 93
Gods, 54, 108. *See also* Myth
  cosmic forces, 107
  nature, 114
  secular, 63
  storm gods, 80
  supernaturals, 103
God-talk. *See also* Apocalyptic;
  Genres; Myth; Prayer; Proverbs;
  Theology; Tragedy
  and absence of God, 45
  ambiguity of, 21, 36, 46
  as apocalyptic, 60
  biblical, 22
  breaking barriers, 48
  brevity of, 20
  caregivers' use of, 3-4
  as catalyst, 43
  as catechism, 43
  context of, 3
  double-sided, 45
  as fence, 45
  as folk-wisdom, 96

God-talk *(continued)*
  genres of, 59
  grammar of, 26
  as grief reaction, 28
  as healing balm, 48
  irony of, 21
  as lament, 60
  as liminal time, 45
  as literary text, 18
  as myth, 9, 43, 63
  offensive, 47
  as ostracization, 42
  as paradox, 21
  paradoxical use of, 35-36, 39
  patterns of, 18
  pastoral purpose, 8, 16
  phenomenon of, 17, 22
  as poetry, 41
  as praise, 11, 46
  as prayer, 60, 134
  purpose of, 45
  religious language, 138
  as similitudes, 40
  as storm-talk, 73
  as superstitions, 111
  as theological language, 67
  as transition, 48
  wisdom of, 46, 63
God-talk phrases
  Do good and God will bless; do bad
    and God will curse, 62
  Every day has a silver lining, 73
  Every day is a gift, 32
  Every thing has a purpose, 52
  God answers prayers, 9
  God bless you, 103
  God didn't do this, 12
  God does not act that way, 138
  God does not do such cruel things to
    us, 16
  God has given us a wonderful,
    precise, orderly world, 53
  God has taken little Susie, 102
  God is a loving parent who controls
    what happens to us, 52
  God is good, 16

God-talk phrases *(continued)*
God is in ... evil and injustice too, 55
God is love, therefore God would never deliberately kill a child, 38
God just doesn't like me any more, 1
God knows what he is doing, 10
God loves me, 11
God must have a reason for this, 29
God must have been with us in that hurricane last week, 8, 139
God remains in control, 46
God took him quickly, 9
God took little Susie from this earth, 19
God took Uncle Harry today, 1
God was just with us that day, I guess, 8
God will get that drunk who killed my boy!, 19, 60
God will get us through this, 108
Has God forgotten me?, 116
Help me Jesus!, 134
Hey, it could be worse, brother, 41
How could such a loving God do such a thing?, 15, 50
I always thought she would live forever, 126
I am at peace with God, 48
I don't know why all this has happened to me but I guess there is some reason for it, 1
I don't know why God selected us to live and others to die, 8
I feel the power of God during thunderstorms, 75
I guess God had a need for Billy, so he took him from us, 139
I have been a good person all of my life, 134
I just knew Joe's drinking would be his downfall, 82
I just placed it in the Lord's hands, 10
I see God in the Littleton tragedy, 12

God-talk phrases *(continued)*
I simply can't cope with such a burden, 5
I thought God was in control, 133
I want to believe that God does not play cat and mouse with us, 28
I was a good person. I went to church on Sunday, 117
I will be given my due someday, 125
If God wanted her to die, then so be it, 10
If God was fair..., 50
If God was ready for the curtain to come down on this final act of mine, 35
If it is my time to go, then it is my time to go, 11
If she would have just given her life to the Lord rather than..., 82
I'll pray for you, 44
I'm glad God had mercy on her and stopped her misery, 10
I'm sorry, 44, 45
Is God ever going to look favorably on me?, 116
Is it rational to believe in a bad God?, 48
It is God's will that you live joyously and fully, 32
It is not God's will that you or any one of God's children should suffer or die, 32
It won't happen to me, 133
Jesus saves, 3
Just when I got my life going again God knocked me down, 19
Look at this precious little gift God has given us, 102
Maybe some good will come of it, 82
My God, my God, why have you forsaken me?, 132
My God would never do that to anyone, 133
Oh God, where are you?, 134
Oh my God!, 18, 60
She is with God, 47

God-talk phrases *(continued)*
She's better off up there now, 10
Surely no good God would cause such an event to occur, 25
That was the way he wanted to go, 9
The Lord will not put on you any more than you can bear, 4, 41, 63
The Lord will take care of you, 4
The Lord wills it, 41
There is a reason for this, and we will understand it one day, 29, 63
This can't happen to me!, 134
This life is so short, but there she can praise God for an eternity, 139
This tragedy...made me realize that I was running away from God, 80
Was God not with those who died in the storms?, 75
What ever happens is God's will, 32
What if God takes people when God wants to?, 140
What kind of God would do such a sinister thing?, 4
When this is over I'll get my heart right with God, 108
Why?, 12
Why, oh Lord?, 122
Why are you doing this to me?, 28
Why do bad things happen to good people?, 51
Why is God doing this to me?, 60
Why is this happening to me?, 19, 50, 117
Yeah, but there are a lot of others hurting worse than me right now, 32, 84
You can't die now!, 134
You'll get yours buddy!, 126
You'll understand this better down the road, 45
Goldberg, David J., 147
Green, Garrett, 36, 69
Grief
 cycle of, 47, 77

Grief *(continued)*
 as fear, 47
 as liminal time, 43
Guilt, 3, 8, 26
 emotions of, 82
Gutierrez, Gustavo, 151

Hall, Douglas John, 148
Hanson, Paul, 119
Hermeneutics, process of, 3
Hero, 132
Holy, 94
Holy Spirit, 66, 80
Hope, 20, 89. *See also* Paradigm
 future hope, 30
 light of, 43
Humphreys, W. Lee, 132
Hymnody, 5, 41, 48, 69, 123

Imagination, 36, 139
 religious, 69
Initiation, 104, 145
 rites of, 43
Irrational thought, 1

Jacob, 50
Jesus, 74, 76, 128, 132
 as God-in-the-flesh, 89
 as myth, 68
 suffering, death, and resurrection of, 64
 suffers, 84
 struggles, 30
 to die, 15
Jesus prayer, 35
Job, 50, 52-52, 74, 76, 87
John of Patmos, 74
Johnson, George, 149
Jonah, 15, 52
Joseph, 63, 76, 83, 132
Jung, Carl, 119. *See also* Jungians
Jungians, 68

Kelsey, Morton, 91
Kitchener, Karen Strohm, 152
Koch, Klaus, 153
Koester, Helmut, 121
Kreeft, Peter, 31, 36, 38, 39
Kushner, Rabbi Harold S., 28, 50

Labouvie-Vief, Gisela, 152
Lament, biblical, 13, 136
Language, 112
 apocalyptic, 111
 A-rational, 92
 discourse of, 58, 65
 emotive, 61
 fantastic, 114
 liturgical, 123
 modern industrial vocabulary, 66
 nonrational, 61
 poetic, 65
 as prayer, 135
 of psychology, 67
 religious, 61-62, 112, 123
 rhetorical, 65
 ritualistic, 117
 of sociology, 67
 theological, 61
 worship, 117
Legalism, 115-116
L'Engle, Madeleine, 34, 140
Lester, Andrew D., 122
Levenson, Jon D., 81, 114
Lewis, C.S., 47
Liderbach, Daniel, 57, 61, 64-67
Literate religion, 115
Living human documents, 41
Love, 143
Luck, 12

Mackenzie, 28
Macquarrie, John, 57
Marty, Martin E., 40, 99, 104
McCullough, Donald, 151
McFague, Sallie, 68

Memes, 96
Metaphor
 in religious language, 69-70
 storms as, 77
Moltmann, Jurgen, 113
Mysterium tremendum, 93
Mystery, 33, 97. *See also* God; Truth
 and the fear of God, 49
 god as, 34
 of life, 30
 realm of, 37
Mystical, realm of, 12
Myth, 18, 49, 60, 63, 91. *See also*
  Theology; Truth
 academic, 34
 as action of the gods, 96
 ancient, 22, 44, 52
 and archaic speech, 102
 Bible stories as, 106
 and counseling, 105
 creation, 107-108
 creation of, 47
 definition of, 101
 developing, 49
 God-talk as, 9, 17, 32
 as history, 97-98
 imagination, 37
 inadequate, 50
 Jesus Christ as, 68, 99-100
 as literary category, 131
 modern, 22
 as mythos, 18, 101
 and origins, 102
 patriarchal, 68
 personal, 48
 as poetry, 97
 post-tragedy, 49
 premodern, 66
 pretragedy, 50
 as science, 97

Neoorthodoxy, 66
Nihilism, 53, 94
Noah, 82
Numinous, 93

Oates, Wayne E., 12, 63
Oral religion, 115
Ostracized, 44
Otto, Rudolf, 37, 93

Paradigm
  Bible as, 69, 78
  of hope, 89
Paradox, 7, 73, 139
Pastoral conversation, 6
Paul, 4, 76, 84, 101, 132
  shipwreck, 83
  trust in God, 5
Perception, personal, 2, 133. See also Sin
Peter, 84, 101, 127-128, 133
Peterson, Eugene H., 39, 140
Piper, O. A., 145
Plato, 96
Prayer, 19, 135-136
  God-talk as, 17
  New Testament, 65
Primitive magic, 35
Primitive religion, 76
Probes, pastoral, 2, 63
Problems, 6-7
Profane, 43, 44
Proverbs, 63
  God-talk as, 17, 20, 49
Providence, 25
Psychoanalysis, as ancient ritual, 104
Psychology, 124. See also Apocalyptic
  enlightenment influenced, 25
  pop-psychology, 29, 34, 94, 101, 127, 151
  as religion, 151
Psychotherapy, 12, 13
Purdue, Leo G., 108

Ra, as evil, 14
Rathunde, Kevin, 152
Rational thought, 1
Ratliffe, J. Bill, 150

Reason, 26
  divine, 1, 29
  philosophical, 5, 25
  rational, 1
  theological, 5
Recovery, spiritual, 2
Reframing, 4
  the issue, 6
Re-mythologization, 68, 105, 118. See also Apocalyptic
Ricouer, Paul, 70
Rituals, 101-104
Robinson, Daniel N., 152
Robinson, Edward, 139
Ruach, 80. See also Holy Spirit
Russell, D.S., 113-114
Ruth, 141

Sacred, 43-44
Salvation, guilt of, 3, 8
Sample, Tex, 113
Sasson, Jack, 81
Satan, 21, 128, 144
  as accuser, 86
  power of, 15
  worship of, 92
Schizophrenia, 126
Schleiermacher, Friederich, 65
Scribal religion, 115
Seminary, 6, 22
Shalom, peace, 14
Short stories, God-talk as, 17
Sin, 99, 133, 154
  of idolatry, 134
  as misperception, 133
  as overdefining of God, 38
  of presumptuousness, 50, 87
  as separation from God, 38
  of victimization, 67
Smith, Huston, 66
Smith, Jonathan Z., 118
Smith, Mark S., 78
Sociology, 12
Sontag, Frederick, 16, 31

Soul, 95
St. Augustine, 33
Stone, Howard W., 13, 58, 63
Subconscious, 140
Sufferers, 2
  and humility, 32
  language of, 3
  pain of, 3
Suffering, 31
  and evil, 145
  as fact of life, 6
  as good, 33
  as joy, 128
  meaning in, 65
  as sacrifice, 101
  as transfiguration, 48
Superstition, 35
Survivors, 2
  response of, 3
Switzer, David K., 77
Symbols, 101

Taylor, Mark C., 147
Temptation, God-given, 4
Terrien, Samuel, 153
Testing, 4
  of faith, 15
Theodicy, 16, 25
  arguments of, 13
  unresolved, 21
Theology
  acceptable, 138
  ambiguity of, 37
  changing, 5, 62
  church's, 141
  competing, 117
  crisis of, 61
  equivalent to God-talk, 57
  everyday, 43
  formal, 136
  functional, 118, 129
  as God-talk, 61
  as hermeneutics, 70
  as imagination, 57

Theology *(continued)*
  implied, 142
  inadequate, 129
  lazy, 54
  liberal, 66
  liberation, 65, 67
  liturgical, 136
  as myth, 37, 57
  natural, 114
  paradox of, 37
  pastoral, 2
  personal, 2, 51
  post-modern, 65, 67
  primitive, 63
  rational, 1, 25, 51
  sufferer's, 154
  tension in, 37
Tillich, Paul, 67
Time
  chronos, 104, 109
  kairos, 104, 109
  liminal, 1, 104
  profane, 104
  of questioning, 123
  sacred, 104
  temporal, 1
Tragedy
  as humiliation, 87
  God involved in, 4
  God-talk as, 17, 19
  physical, 22
  psychological, 22
  surviving end of, 25
  as trial, 44
Truth
  mystery and myth of, 36
  as storms of life, 39

Ulanov, Ann and Barry, 139
Unconscious, 95
Utopia, state of, 7

Vitz, Paul C., 143
von Rad, Gerhard, 149

Weal and woe, 29, 49, 100
Weisel, Elie, 54
Wellhausen, Julius, 120
Wells, David F., 146
Westermann, Claus, 108
Wimberly, Edward P., 106
Wisdom, 95-96
  as apocalyptic, 118
  as archetype, 20
  as faith development, 144
  as logos, 96

Wisdom *(continued)*
  as mythos, 96
  as reverence of God, 49
Wisdom literature, 63, 109
  as paradigm, 22
Wiser, Artur, 151

Zenger, Erich, 99
Zurheide, Jeffrey R., 148
Zwerner, Jane Mary, 48

Order a copy of this book with this form or online at:
http://www.haworthpressinc.com/store/product.asp?sku=4607

A THEOLOGY OF GOD-TALK
The Language of the Heart

_____ in hardbound at $39.95 (ISBN: 0-7890-1514-5)
_____ in softbound at $19.95 (ISBN: 0-7890-1515-3)

COST OF BOOKS_____	❏ **BILL ME LATER:** ($5 service charge will be added)
OUTSIDE USA/CANADA/ MEXICO: ADD 20%_____	(Bill-me option is good on US/Canada/Mexico orders only; not good to jobbers, wholesalers, or subscription agencies.)
POSTAGE & HANDLING_____ (US: $4.00 for first book & $1.50 for each additional book) Outside US: $5.00 for first book & $2.00 for each additional book)	❏ Check here if billing address is different from shipping address and attach purchase order and billing address information. Signature_____
SUBTOTAL_____	❏ **PAYMENT ENCLOSED:** $_____
in Canada: add 7% GST_____	❏ **PLEASE CHARGE TO MY CREDIT CARD.**
STATE TAX_____ (NY, OH & MIN residents, please add appropriate local sales tax)	❏ Visa ❏ MasterCard ❏ AmEx ❏ Discover ❏ Diner's Club ❏ Eurocard ❏ JCB Account # _____
FINAL TOTAL_____ (If paying in Canadian funds, convert using the current exchange rate, UNESCO coupons welcome.)	Exp. Date_____ Signature_____

Prices in US dollars and subject to change without notice.

NAME_____
INSTITUTION_____
ADDRESS_____
CITY_____
STATE/ZIP_____
COUNTRY_____ COUNTY (NY residents only)_____
TEL_____ FAX_____
E-MAIL_____
May we use your e-mail address for confirmations and other types of information? ❏ Yes ❏ No
We appreciate receiving your e-mail address and fax number. Haworth would like to e-mail or fax special discount offers to you, as a preferred customer. **We will never share, rent, or exchange your e-mail address or fax number.** We regard such actions as an invasion of your privacy.

Order From Your Local Bookstore or Directly From
The Haworth Press, Inc.
10 Alice Street, Binghamton, New York 13904-1580 • USA
TELEPHONE: 1-800-HAWORTH (1-800-429-6784) / Outside US/Canada: (607) 722-5857
FAX: 1-800-895-0582 / Outside US/Canada: (607) 722-6362
E-mail: getinfo@haworthpressinc.com

PLEASE PHOTOCOPY THIS FORM FOR YOUR PERSONAL USE.
www.HaworthPress.com

BOF02

FORTHCOMING BOOKS FROM HAWORTH RELIGION, MINISTRY, AND SPIRITUALITY

CHRONIC PAIN
Biomedical and Spiritual Approaches
Harold G. Koenig, MD
Provides essential information about how to reduce physical pain and explores techniques for improving people's ability to cope with it. The author, who suffers from chronic pain and disability himself, explores ways to cope with low back pain, fibromyalgia, rheumatologic pain, headaches, the pain of multiple sclerosis, and more.
$24.95 soft. ISBN: 0-7890-1639-7.
$49.95 hard. ISBN: 0-7890-1638-9.
Available Winter 2002/2003. Approx. 299 pp. with Index.

COUNSELING FOR THE SOUL IN DISTRESS
REVISED EDITION!
What Every Religious Counselor Should Know About Emotional and Mental Illness, Second Edition
Richard W. Roukema, MD, FAPA
Updated with new information on genetics, brain scans, heredity, developmental concerns, new medications, and stress, it suggests ways for clergy to assist their congregants suffering from these illnesses.
$29.95 soft. ISBN: 0-7890-1630-3.
$49.95 hard. ISBN: 0-7890-1629-X.
Available Winter 2002/2003. Approx. 284 pp. with Index.

INTEGRATING SPIRIT AND PSYCHE
Using Women's Narratives in Psychotherapy
Mary Pat Henehan, DMin
In this extraordinary collection, women bare their souls, reflecting on self-enhancement and growth, on discrediting negative family scripts, on seeing through demeaning cultural messages, on living in the modern world, on their wildness, wisdom, spirituality, and a great deal more!
$24.95 soft. ISBN: 0-7890-1210-3.
$39.95 hard. ISBN: 0-7890-1209-X.
Available Fall 2002. Approx. 221 pp. with Index.

PASTORAL CARE FOR POST-TRAUMATIC STRESS DISORDER
Healing the Shattered Soul
Daléne C. Fuller Rogers, MDiv
This vital book is an overview of the nature of post-traumatic stress disorder (PTSD). It examines the causes, manifestations, and problems of PTSD as they relate to a person socially, spiritually, emotionally, physically, and psychologically. It provides the practical means to support clients through their healing process while maintaining their spiritual grounding.
$19.95 soft. ISBN: 0-7890-1542-0.
$29.95 hard. ISBN: 0-7890-1541-2.
Available Summer 2002. Approx. 135 pp. with Index.

A PRACTICAL GUIDE TO HOSPITAL MINISTRY
Healing Ways
Junietta Baker McCall, DMin
This excellent resource will help you make a shift toward a knowledge and skill-based ministry that both incorporates and goes beyond current training approaches. It also provides vital resources for hospital ministry, including job descriptions, discussions of various types of hospital ministries, scope-of-practice statements, pastoral care brochures and request forms, orientation checklists, sample religious preference codes, and a list of typical counseling problems.
$34.95 soft. ISBN: 0-7890-1212-X.
$59.95 hard. ISBN: 0-7890-1211-1.
Available Summer 2002. Approx. 352 pp. with Index.

RELIGIOUS THEORIES OF PERSONALITY AND PSYCHOTHERAPY
East Meets West
Edited by R. Paul Olson, MDiv, PhD
Clinical practitioners of different Eastern and Western religious traditions examine the same clinical case, offering insights, interventions, and explanations of transformation and healing. This practical approach allows you to explore broader issues of personality theory and psychology from the perspectives of various spiritual traditions.
$49.95 soft. ISBN: 0-7890-1237-5.
$89.95 hard. ISBN: 0-7890-1236-7.
Available Spring 2002. Approx. 420 pp. with Index.

WHEN THE CAREGIVER BECOMES THE PATIENT
A Journey from a Mental Disorder to Recovery and Compassionate Insight
**Daniel L. Langford, DMin,
and Emil J. Authelet**
A step-by-step guide to the healing and recovery process, mixing the insight of a health care professional with the fear and suffering of a patient. It details the caregiver's renewed appreciation for the human spirit through a profound connection with his or her client.
$24.95 soft. ISBN: 0-7890-1294-4.
$39.95 hard. ISBN: 0-7890-1293-6.
Available Spring 2002. Approx. 216 pp. with Index.

CALL OUR TOLL-FREE NUMBER: 1-800-429-6784
US & Canada only / 8am–5pm ET; Monday–Friday
Outside US/Canada: + 607-722-5857
FAX YOUR ORDER TO US: 1-800-895-0582
Outside US/Canada: + 607-771-0012
E-MAIL YOUR ORDER TO US:
orders@HaworthPressInc.com
VISIT OUR WEB SITE AT:
http://www.HaworthPress.com

The Haworth Pastoral Press®
An imprint of The Haworth Press, Inc.
10 Alice Street
Binghamton, New York 13904-1580 USA

MORE PUBLISHED BOOKS FROM
HAWORTH RELIGION, MINISTRY & SPIRITUALITY

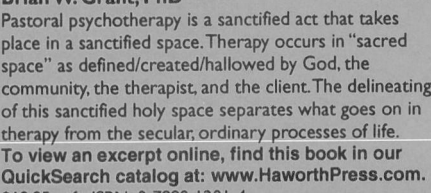

A THEOLOGY FOR PASTORAL PSYCHOTHERAPY
God's Play in Sacred Spaces
Brian W. Grant, PhD

Pastoral psychotherapy is a sanctified act that takes place in a sanctified space. Therapy occurs in "sacred space" as defined/created/hallowed by God, the community, the therapist, and the client. The delineating of this sanctified holy space separates what goes on in therapy from the secular, ordinary processes of life.
To view an excerpt online, find this book in our QuickSearch catalog at: www.HaworthPress.com.
$19.95 soft. ISBN: 0-7890-1201-4.
$29.95 hard. ISBN: 0-7890-1200-6. 2001. 238 pp. with Index.

WU WEI, NEGATIVITY, AND DEPRESSION
The Principle of Non-Trying in the Practice of Pastoral Care
Siroj Sorajjakool, PhD

This significant book offers a comprehensive discussion of depression, including biological causes, psychosocial theories, standard treatments of the past and present, and pastoral care of depressed persons.
To view an excerpt online, find this book in our QuickSearch catalog at: www.HaworthPress.com.
$17.95 soft. ISBN: 0-7890-1094-1.
$49.95 hard. ISBN: 0-7890-1093-3. 2001. 184 pp. with Index.

AGING AND SPIRITUALITY
Spiritual Dimensions of Aging Theory, Research, Practice, and Policy
Edited by David O. Moberg, PhD

By integrating spiritual issues into the theoretical framework of social gerontology, this book will help you understand the scientific foundations, practical applications, and public policy implications of spirituality for older adults.
To view an excerpt online, find this book in our QuickSearch catalog at: www.HaworthPress.com.
$24.95 soft. ISBN: 0-7890-0939-0.
$49.95 hard. ISBN: 0-7890-0938-2. 2001. 250 pp. with Index.

FAITH, SPIRITUALITY, AND MEDICINE
Toward the Making of the Healing Practitioner
Dana E. King, MD

"THIS IS A BOOK THAT WILL LEAD US DOWN THE RIGHT PATH TO HEALING, HOLISTIC CARE."
—Resources Hotline
$15.95 soft. ISBN: 0-7890-1115-8.
$49.95 hard. ISBN: 0-7890-0724-X. 2000. 126 pp. with Index.

THE PASTOR'S GUIDE TO PSYCHOLOGICAL DISORDERS AND TREATMENTS
W. Brad Johnson, PhD, and William L. Johnson, Ph

"These authors have recognized the significant presence of mental illness . . . and the role of the clergy in respecting it, recognizing it, and reachir out to people suffering various forms of mental illness."
—Resources Hotline
$24.95 soft. ISBN: 0-7890-1111-5.
$49.95 hard. ISBN: 0-7890-0712-6.
2000. 240 pp. with Index.

SHARED GRACE
Therapists and Clergy Working Together
Marion Bilich, PhD, Susan Bonfiglio, MSW, and Steven D. Carlson, MDiv

"What makes this effort unique is that the authors are a social worker, a therapist, and a member of the clergy who have collaborated to help a patient recover from extensive childhood trauma."
—Journal of Social Work Education
$24.95 soft. ISBN: 0-7890-1110-7.
$49.95 hard. ISBN: 0-7890-0878-5.
2000. 230 pp. with Index.

BROKEN BODIES, HEALING HEARTS
Reflections of a Hospital Chaplain
Gretchen W. TenBrook

"Provides insight into the experiences of hospital patients. REVEALS THE IMPORTANT WORK THAT CHAPLAINS ARE CALLED TO DO and how faith can overcome human frailties."
—Interpreter
$19.95 soft. ISBN: 0-7890-0852-1.
$49.95 hard. ISBN: 0-7890-0851-3.
2000. 172 pp. with Index.

SPIRITUAL CARE FOR CHILDREN LIVING IN SPECIALIZED SETTINGS
Breathing Underwater
Michael F. Friesen, MDiv

"Offers resources for learning about a variety of religions, as well as techniques and methods to create a common language and framework for interventions with children and teens in care facilities."
—Journal of Christian Nursing
$19.95 soft. ISBN: 0-7890-0630-8.
$39.95 hard. ISBN: 0-7890-0629-4.
2000. 150 pp. with Index.

CALL OUR TOLL-FREE NUMBER: 1-800-429-6784
US & Canada only / 8am–5pm ET; Monday–Friday
Outside US/Canada: + 607-722-5857

FAX YOUR ORDER TO US: 1-800-895-0582
Outside US/Canada: + 607-771-0012

E-MAIL YOUR ORDER TO US:
orders@HaworthPressInc.com

VISIT OUR WEB SITE AT:
http://www.HaworthPress.com

WE'RE ONLINE!
VISIT OUR WEB SITE AT:
http://www.HaworthPress.com

FORTHCOMING AND RECENTLY PUBLISHED BOOKS FROM HAWORTH RELIGION, MINISTRY & SPIRITUALITY

A THEOLOGY OF GOD-TALK
The Language of the Heart
J. Timothy Allen, MDiv, MA
Probes the meaning behind phrases like "It must have been God's will" and "The Lord took Uncle Harry." This sensitive, original book demonstrates the ways that God-talk moves the sufferer through the grief and doubt of the crisis.
$19.95 soft. ISBN: 0-7890-1515-3.
$39.95 hard. ISBN: 0-7890-1514-5.
2002. Available now. 189 pp. with Index.

FAMILY ABUSE AND THE BIBLE
The Scriptural Perspective
Aimee K. Cassiday-Shaw, MA
This unique volume reconciles a biblical interpretation of marriage with the reality of domestic violence. It combines close biblical exegesis with psychological insight into the effects of verbal, sexual, physical, and spiritual abuse.
$19.95 soft. ISBN: 0-7890-1577-3.
$49.95 hard. ISBN: 0-7890-1576-5.
2002. Available now. 144 pp. with Index.

BIOETHICS FROM A FAITH PERSPECTIVE
Ethics in Health Care for the Twenty-First Century
Jack T. Hanford, MDiv, MA, ThD
Since almost all textbooks in bioethics omit the religious dimension of life (even though the field was inspired and stimulated by religious scholars at Princeton and Yale), this is an indispensable volume. It is the perfect supplement to the existing literature on bioethics.
To view an excerpt online, find this book in our QuickSearch catalog at: www.HaworthPress.com.
$19.95 soft. ISBN: 0-7890-1510-2.
$49.95 hard. ISBN: 0-7890-1509-9.
2002. Available now. 150 pp. with Index.

FACULTY: ORDER YOUR NO-RISK EXAM COPY TODAY!
Send us your examination copy order on your stationery; indicate course title, enrollment, and course start date. We will ship and bill on a 60-day examination basis, and cancel your invoice if you decide to adopt! We will always bill at the lowest available price, such as our special "5+ text price." Please remember to order softcover where available. (We cannot provide examination copies of books not published by The Haworth Press, Inc., or its imprints.) (Outside US/Canada, a proforma invoice will be sent upon receipt of your request and must be paid in advance of shipping. A full refund will be issued with proof of adoption.)

PASTORAL COUNSELING
A Gestalt Approach
Ward A. Knights, Jr., BA, MDiv, STM, DD
This book explains how the basic goals of Gestalt work (to achieve spontaneity and expressiveness and to move toward personal authenticity) will help you and your congregation move toward realizing your God-given potential.
To view an excerpt online, find this book in our QuickSearch catalog at: www.HaworthPress.com.
$24.95 soft. ISBN: 0-7890-1532-3.
$39.95 hard. ISBN: 0-7890-1531-5.
2002. Available now. 126 pp. with Index.

CHRIST-CENTERED THERAPY
Empowering the Self
Russ Harris, PhD, MDiv, LCSW
Provides exercises and visual aids to help both client and counselor, including worksheets, a "parts map" for client and counselor to use collaboratively, case studies, and a clinical outline listing the interventions in sequence. This book is essential for Christian counselors and for non-Christian counselors who are seeking more effective ways to treat Christian clients.
To view an excerpt online, find this book in our QuickSearch catalog at: www.HaworthPress.com.
$24.95 soft. ISBN: 0-7890-1228-6.
$49.95 hard. ISBN: 0-7890-1227-8. 2001. 284 pp. with Index.

A WOLF IN THE ATTIC
The Legacy of a Hidden Child of the Holocaust
Sophia Richman, PhD
This book follows the author's life as she gradually becomes able to reclaim her past, to understand its impact on her life and the choices she has made, and to heal a part of herself that she had so long been taught to deny.
To view an excerpt online, find this book in our QuickSearch catalog at: www.HaworthPress.com.
$22.95 soft. ISBN: 0-7890-1550-1.
$49.95 hard. ISBN: 0-7890-1549-8.
2001, 275 pp. with 28-page photo section.

PASTORAL CARE TO MUSLIMS
Building Bridges
Neville A. Kirkwood, DMin
Addresses the fact that more and more often pastoral care workers are encountering Muslims in hospitals. This is the guidebook you need to provide the spiritual support these patients are able to accept—support that doesn't conflict with their religious affiliations.
$17.95 soft. ISBN: 0-7890-1477-7.
$34.95 hard. ISBN: 0-7890-1476-9. 2001. 150 pp. with Index.

The Haworth Pastoral Press®
An imprint of The Haworth Press, Inc.
10 Alice Street, Binghamton, New York 13904-1580 USA

"MARTHA, MARTHA"
How Christians Worry
Elaine Leong Eng, MD
$14.95 soft. ISBN: 0-7890-0866-1.
$39.95 hard. ISBN: 0-7890-0865-3.
2000. 134 pp. with Index. **Translated into Chinese.**

THE OBSESSIVE-COMPULSIVE DISORDER
Pastoral Care for the Road to Change
Robert M. Collie, ThD

 Over 225 Pages!

$19.95 soft. ISBN: 0-7890-0862-9.
$54.95 hard. ISBN: 0-7890-0707-X.
1999. 267 pp. with Index.

WAYS OF THE DESERT
Becoming Holy Through Difficult Times
William E. Kraft, PhD
$19.95 soft. ISBN: 0-7890-0860-2.
$49.95 hard. ISBN: 0-7890-0859-9.
1999. 166 pp. with Index.

LIFE CYCLE
Psychological and Theological Perceptions
Richard Dayringer, ThD
$22.95 soft. ISBN: 0-7890-0905-6.
$54.95 hard. ISBN: 0-7890-0171-3. 1999. 177 pp. with Index.

CARING FOR A LOVED ONE WITH ALZHEIMER'S DISEASE
A Christian Perspective
Elizabeth T. Hall, BS
$18.95 soft. ISBN: 0-7890-0873-4.
$54.95 hard. ISBN: 0-7890-0872-6. 1999. 150 pp. with Index

THE PASTORAL CARE OF CHILDREN
Daniel H. Grossoehme, BCC
$21.95 soft. ISBN: 0-7890-0605-7.
$74.95 hard. ISBN: 0-7890-0604-9. 1999. 152 pp. with Index

CARING FOR PEOPLE FROM BIRTH TO DEATH
Edited by James E. Hightower, Jr., EdD
$19.95 soft. ISBN: 0-7890-0572-7.
$74.95 hard. ISBN: 0-7890-0571-9. 1999. 204 pp. with Index

CALL OUR TOLL-FREE NUMBER: 1-800-429-6784
US & Canada only / 8am-5pm ET; Monday-Friday
Outside US/Canada: + 607-722-5857

FAX YOUR ORDER TO US: 1-800-895-0582
Outside US/Canada: + 607-771-0012

E-MAIL YOUR ORDER TO US:
orders@HaworthPressInc.com

VISIT OUR WEB SITE AT:
http://www.HaworthPress.com

Take 20% Off Each Book!

WE'RE ONLINE!
VISIT OUR WEB SITE AT:
http://www.HaworthPress.com

Order Today and Save!

TITLE	ISBN	REGULAR PRICE	20%-OFF PRICE

- Discount available only in US, Canada, and Mexico and not available in conjunction with any other offer.
- Individual orders outside US, Canada, and Mexico must be prepaid by check, credit card, or money order.
- In Canada: Add 7% for GST after postage & handling. Residents of Newfoundland, Nova Scotia, and New Brunswick, add an additional 8% for province tax.
- MN, NY, and OH residents: Add appropriate local sales tax.

Please complete information below or tape your business card in this area.

NAME_____

ADDRESS_____
_____

CITY_____

STATE_____ ZIP_____

COUNTRY_____

COUNTY (NY residents only)_____

TEL _____ FAX _____
[Please type or print clearly!]

E-MAIL_____
May we use your e-mail address for confirmations and other types of information?
( ) Yes ( ) No. We appreciate receiving your e-mail address and fax number. Haworth would like to e-mail or fax special discount offers to you, as a preferred customer. We will never **share, rent, or exchange** your e-mail address or fax number. We regard such actions as an invasion of your privacy.

POSTAGE AND HANDLING:
If your book total is:	Add
up to $29.95	$5.00
$30.00 - $49.99	$6.00
$50.00 - $69.99	$7.00
$70.00 - $89.99	$8.00
$90.00 - $109.99	$9.00
$110.00 - $129.99	$10.00
$130.00 - $149.99	$11.00
$150.00 and up	$12.00

- US orders will be shipped via UPS; Outside US orders will be shipped via Book Printed Matter. For shipments via other delivery services, contact Haworth for details. Based on US dollars. Booksellers: Call for freight charges. • If paying in Canadian funds, please use the current exchange rate to convert total to Canadian dollars. • Payment in UNESCO coupons welcome. • Please allow 3-4 weeks for delivery after publication.
- Prices and discounts subject to change without notice. • Discount not applicable on books priced under $15.00.

❏ **BILL ME LATER** ($5 service charge will be added).
(Bill-me option is not available on orders outside US/Canada/Mexico. Service charge is waived for booksellers/wholesalers/jobbers.)

Signature_____

❏ **PAYMENT ENCLOSED** _____
(Payment must be in US or Canadian dollars by check or money order drawn on a US or Canadian bank.)

❏ **PLEASE CHARGE TO MY CREDIT CARD:**
❏ AmEx ❏ Diners Club ❏ Discover ❏ Eurocard ❏ JCB ❏ Master Card ❏ Visa

Account #_____ Exp Date _____

Signature_____

May we open a confidential credit card account for you for possible future purchases? ( ) Yes ( ) No

The Haworth Press, Inc.
10 Alice Street, Binghamton, New York 13904-1580 USA